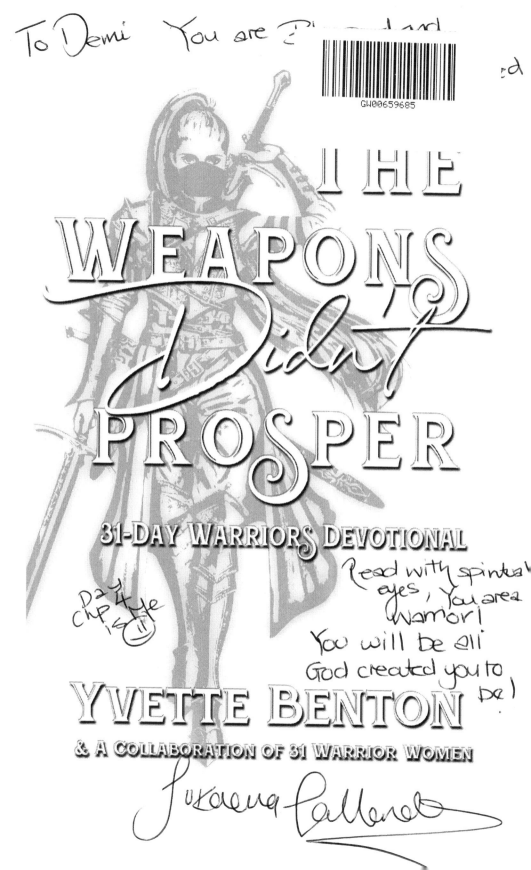

To Demi   You are ?'

GW00659685

THE WEAPONS Didn't PROSPER

31-DAY WARRIORS DEVOTIONAL

Read with spiritual eyes, You are a Warrior!
You will be all God created you to be!

Day 4
Chp ? ?

YVETTE BENTON

& A COLLABORATION OF 31 WARRIOR WOMEN

The Weapons Didn't Prosper: 31-Day Warriors Devotional

Help for The Helpmeet, Inc.

Kennesaw, GA

Assisted by Global Destiny Enterprises, LLC

Cover Design by Angela Mills Camper of Dezign Pro Printing & Graphics

First Printing, 2022

ISBN: 978-1-7346335-3-5

Table of Contents

Introduction

God requires that we establish ourselves in righteousness. What is righteousness? Getting yourself in line with God's will and conforming to His order. **As the Word of God is written in Isaiah 54:14:**

"You shall establish yourself in righteousness (rightness, in conformity with God's will and order): you shall be far from even the thought of oppression *or* destruction, for you shall not fear, and from terror, for it shall not come near you" (AMPC).

The Hebrew word for "establish" means firm, stable, and fixed. If you want to be fixed in God in this season, you must be righteous.

In this season, we must stabilize ourselves and be ready. To be prepared, we must establish ourselves. In the process of doing so, things will be set in order, and we will begin to understand the order of God. We must seek first and understand righteousness.

"But seek (aim at and strive after) first of all His kingdom and His righteousness (His way of doing and being right), and then all these things taken together will be given you besides" (Matthew 6:33, AMPC).

We must distance ourselves from even the thought of oppression and destruction. Inevitably, oppression causes destruction. Isaiah Chapter 54 says we have to be far from it. But what do we do if oppression and destruction are nearby? We must use our swords (the Word of God) and cut them off. Demonic assignments are meant to pull us close to oppression and destruction, but God's Word tells us to cut them off. Then, we shall not fear terror, for it shall not come near us.

We must set ourselves up to understand God's will and order so things like oppression, destruction, and fear are removed from our lives. No terror can touch us. Nothing can hinder us. It shall not come near us. If the Bible says it shall not come near us and it's near us, what are we going to do?

When we establish ourselves and are firm, we also understand our rights. Knowing our rights is critical to our success because we will command and demand to be free. We will cut off oppression, destruction, and fear to make sure they do not come anywhere near us. Use your sword (the Word of God). Know your rights. Declare, "I know my rights. I am being established in this season. So, I am not going to accept destruction, fear, or oppression.

"Behold, they may gather together *and* stir up strife, but it is not from Me. Whoever stirs up strife against you shall fall *and* surrender to you" (Isaiah 54:15, AMPC).

The word, "behold" means to see and look around. People may gather and stir up strife. Memories congregate in your mind and stir up strife. If something stirs up strife, God is saying it is not from Him. If people are gathering, causing confusion in your life, family, and marriage, it is not from God. Push it away and cut it off. The Word declares whoever stirs up strife against us, God's people, shall fall and surrender to us.

We are warriors, so anything that comes our way must bow to the name of Jesus. It has to surrender to us. So, how do we make sure anything that is causing strife surrenders to us? Again, we must understand our rights, be established in righteousness, and cut off anything that is outside of God's will. If strife, destruction, oppression, fear, or terror are in your life, cut them off. We must know who we are. When we see and experience strife, we have to do something about it. Unfortunately, in the body of Christ, too often, we see issues God says should not be there. But we sit back and watch them. We sit back and complain, whine, or cry. That is not what the Bible says we should do. It says we do not have to understand what's going on. We do not have to accept what's happening, but whatever is causing the strife must surrender. We are representatives of the Word and body of Christ. We must know whose we are and who we are.

When we recognize we are warriors, we quickly know we are not bound by foolishness. We have the authority in the spirit realm. God wants us to open our eyes and see what's around us. Sometimes we are blind in the spirit; we're not taking notice of what the enemy is doing. We are not taking notice of what he is building up. He is building up strife around us. God is saying look: pay attention. In this season, we cannot be blind in the spirit. Take the blinders off and look at what satan is doing. We must know how to deal with him in the spirit. God tells us to behold.

"Behold, I have created the smith who blows on the fire of coals and who produces a weapon for its purpose, and I have created the devastator to destroy" (Isaiah 56:16, AMPC).

A smith is someone who is locked and loaded, someone who is a holder of a weapon. A smith is a craftsman, a skillful person who destroys, a warrior. God created the smith, the warrior. He created someone who knows how to use a weapon. The Bible declares that when the kingdom suffers violence, the violent take it by force (Matthew 11:12). When I look around, the kingdom is suffering violence. What we do not see enough of is God's people, the violent, taking it by force. We need some smiths. God is calling up some smiths, some crafty people, some skillful people who know how to destroy the works of the enemy, who know how to be warriors in the spirit. God has assigned warring angels to His warriors to destroy the plans of the enemy.

But no weapon that is formed against you shall prosper,

and every tongue that shall rise against you in judgment you shall show to be wrong. This [peace, righteousness, security, triumph over opposition] is the heritage of the servants of the Lord [those in whom the ideal Servant of the Lord is reproduced]; this is the righteousness *or* the vindication which they obtain from Me [this is that which I impart to them as their justification], says the Lord. (Isaiah 54:17)

Isaiah 54:17 is a powerful scripture we must commit to studying, understanding, and memorizing. Use this scripture with meaning and power.

What weapons have been formed against you? What weapons have been formed against your family? What weapons have been formed against your marriage? What weapons have been formed against your health? What weapons have been formed against your children? What weapons have been formed against your bloodline? Isaiah 54:17 is not an unfamiliar scripture, but we act as if it is. It says no weapon formed against you shall prosper. Look around. Unfortunately, what I have been seeing is weapons prospering. But what does the Bible say?

No weapon that's formed against you will prosper. Do you know why it's prospering despite what the Bible says? Because we're not raising the sword. Do you know why it's prospering? Because we don't know what we have been given in the Word. Do you know why it's prospering? Because we are too busy whining and complaining, instead of raising up swords. Weapons are prospering because we are giving the enemy our authority. This must stop! No weapon formed against us shall prosper.

No weapon formed against your family, children, husband, or marriage shall prosper. Any tongue that rises against you in judgment will be shown to be in the wrong and exposed. We can't be concerned about what people think because we are warriors, not worriers. If a tongue is raised against you, it will not be of concern because people will talk when we start doing what warriors do. We just won't listen; we can't change what God says because of what someone else might say. The question is, what does God say? What does the Word say? The Word says if the weapon is formed against us, it will not prosper. It is our duty to make sure it doesn't prosper. It is our duty to raise our swords of the Spirit. God will deal with the tongues that rise against us. Our only concern should be making sure we stand up knowing no weapon—no weapon of the tongue, no weapon of confusion will prosper.

We will triumph over opposition because we will not be concerned about it. Vengeance belongs to the Lord. God will repay, which allows us to operate in His peace. When we understand our authority, this is actually a sign of peace. And when we understand our authority, we get aggressive in the Spirit because God is saying when the kingdom suffers violence, the violent take it by force (Matthew 11:12). People think when you go into spiritual warfare you are always angry and frustrated, but that is not the case. Peace, righteousness, and security, belong to the children of God.

When we realize a weapon is forming, we carry the peace and authority of God to declare: "No weapon is allowed to prosper. No weapon is allowed to come forth in my life, money, or family. When we belong to God, it is our heritage to have peace. Even when we know the weapons are formed, we can have peace because we are confident they won't prosper.

It can be frustrating when all you hear about is the opposition in people's life. We are called to show them Jesus and the Word. Our duty is to show them what God said. It is the heritage of the servants of the Lord. Are you serving the Lord? Are you a servant of the Lord? Are you a saint? Do you belong to the body of Christ? If you do, if you are a servant of the Lord, you will triumph over it all. The position belongs to you. It's yours. When you're a servant of the Lord, God wants to reproduce you. Warriors reproduce warriors and bring others with them.

When the Lord is reproduced in our words and actions, people notice as we triumph over the opposition. This is the righteousness or the vindication, which they obtained from God. When you know who you are, stand up against injustice; know you are the righteousness of God, and understand the weapon. The weapon won't prosper because we will use the Word against it. We will decree and declare we are overcomers.

When we hide the Word in our hearts, refuse to sin against God, and consciously decide to respond like Jesus, the weapons formed against us won't prosper. They may form, but they won't prosper. When we respond like Christ, no weapons will prosper. When we speak the Word, weapons don't prosper; when we stand firm in the Word, weapons don't prosper. God is imparting into us the knowledge we need, so the weapons won't prosper in our lives, bloodlines, or finances. No weapon of sickness, disease, confusion, bitterness, anger, poverty, lust, or perversion will prosper.

This is how God gets to justify us. When we can identify the weapon, we know it's not going to prosper because we will speak the Word. We will decree and declare the Word and respond like Jesus. The weapon will only prosper if we do things outside of God's will and don't understand what God says in His Word. If we let the enemy rise up and don't use the sword of the Spirit to cut him off, respond like God, and love the unlovable, the weapon will defeat us. Forgive; shut down the assignment of bitterness and anger; respond like Christ, and the weapons will not prosper. Give, and it shall be given unto you. Don't hold on to poverty and lack. If you do, you won't release the seed in your hand. Do what God says to conquer the weapons.

God is raising up warriors who understand weapons and will take their authority and rightful places. Warriors triumph over opposition and understand who they are in Christ. Warriors study the Word and show themselves approved. God's Word says He will teach our hands to war and our fingers to fight. So, we can't wimp out and say it doesn't take all that because it does. It takes all that to keep the weapon from prospering against our marriages, finances, and bloodline. God is teaching His warriors how to use their weapons skillfully. And to do so, we must use the Word. Rolling over and playing dead in this season will not work.

We have destinies to fulfill and families to get saved and delivered. Our children must be saved and delivered. We have a generation to fight for; we must raise the next generation to be warriors. Weapons will form, but it's how we respond that determines what will prosper. Check how you respond when weapons are formed. Are you the reason why they are prospering? If so, change the way you respond. We must change our mentality to react properly and according to the Word of God.

Is God raising you up to understand how to use weapons of warfare? The weapons are not carnal, so when something rises up against you, you must know what to do. A soft answer turns away wrath; therefore, you must know how to use your sword: give a soft answer because it turns away wrath. When we understand the Word, we're not aggressive in the natural; we're aggressive in the spirit realm.

This 31-day devotional shares testimonies of women in my mentoring group the Helpmeet Army. They are Helpmeet warrior women who refused to allow weapons to prosper in their lives. Each day, you will read how the enemy tried to hinder them and how God brought them through. You will also find scriptures to read and warfare prayers to declare. The reflection questions will stimulate your thoughts and allow you to journal how you can use the Word of God and these testimonies to overcome weapons in your own life. Become a warrior in the spirit by using this powerful resource to shut down the enemy and his assignments.

Yvette Benton

Day 1
In the Stillness
by Amina Aboki-Thompson

"Be still and know (recognize & understand) that I am God. I will be exalted among the nations. I will be exalted in the earth" (Psalm 46:10, AMPC).

It was the summer of 2018. There I was on the floor of my bedroom having an emotional meltdown. I had tried everything possible to take my pain away, but nothing seemed to be working. My head felt too big for my body as if it was about to explode. I couldn't understand what was happening to me, but I remember screaming the words,

"God, where are You? Why me? Are You even real? Why is all this happening to me?"

My marriage was falling apart; my child was not doing well in school, and my credit card debt was through the roof. How did I even get here? How did we get here? But in the noise surrounded by love trying to calm me down, I heard, "I am here. I have always been here. Be still."

Something about those words calmed my anxiety, and I was able to fall asleep. I woke up with the same emotion threatening to reoccur, but the words "Be still" resounded in my mind louder and louder. Still?! What does that mean? I didn't know how to be still. For a long time since my father died, somehow, I had taken charge of so much of my family's affairs. At times, I had no clue what I was doing, but I felt I was in control of making sure my mom and siblings were okay. Control—the enemy of stillness! This became a learned behavior for me. I learned how to say the right words to get the responses I wanted. Coupled with control, I was now also operating in manipulation. So, how could I be still when all I knew how to do was control the outcome of things? Sometimes, we look down on others for making bad decisions failing to realize certain behaviors start with the right motives. Then, the deceiver of the brethren uses our good to trick us and take us out of alignment with God. As I heard someone say, "It can be a good thing, but is it a God thing?"

Little did I know the Lord was preparing me for more. It just didn't come as I had expected, wrapped up in a red bow, the perfect marriage, the perfect children, and the perfect job. It came wrapped in disruptions, chaos, heartache, betrayal, and pain. Somehow, in the midst of all this, there was One greater than myself offering me hope and peace. I tried so hard and too long to resist it. I was used to the routine of church, but something about this moment let me realize I could not play games anymore; I had to choose something different. I had to choose God's way or potentially face an emotional breakdown. So I started to embark on the journey to His stillness.

The Bible says in Psalm 46:10, "Be still and know that I am God." But what does that mean? Growing up in a Christian home, I always knew God. From a very young age, we had to read our Bible every day after school, and as much as I hated it, it was now a routine for me with no lasting impact on my life. Little did I know God had greater plans for me, but they required I cease from striving and fighting my way. It meant I had to let go of my perfect girl image and acknowledge my life was in chaos. I needed to loosen up, trust Him, find Him, and surrender to him, even in the midst of the hurt, disappointment, and agony I felt. I had to lay my arms down and realize I couldn't make this journey called life on my own and God was my refuge. He was my safety net.

I began to find solace in reading the Word, worshipping, listening to sermons, prayers and taking long walks to have conversations with Him. Initially, it made no sense. It wasn't like anything I had seen or used. However, it felt true; the love I felt from Him was undeniably beautiful. I surrounded myself with a community of people who could help me on my journey, and it wasn't easy being vulnerable. I cried many times, still wanting to control the outcomes of my life, but I was exhausted after every failed attempt.

Through the chaos that surrounded me, Psalm 46:10 resounded in my soul as the Lord quieted the storms surrounding me within His love (Zephaniah 3:17). I had to cease going into prayer with my long list of complaints because God will do as He will with me. I struggled, cried, learned how to wave my white flag, take corrections, take instructions, and fight differently. Suddenly, I began to feel a wave of peace, and the things that mattered before no longer mattered anymore. With the help of the Holy Spirit, I found a place of rest, trust, and confidence in knowing who I was in God—fearfully and wonderfully made! No longer could the enemy define me, deceive me, and steal my identity as a daughter of the Most High God.

Reflection Questions

1. What areas in your life are you attempting to control?

2. To what degree are you fighting the right way and with the right weapons?

Warfare Prayer

Awesome God, ruler of heaven and the earth, You alone are exalted above every circumstance I face in life. I desire to lay my burdens down and trust You. Teach me, Lord, how to stop striving and put my trust in You. Your Word says You have given us power and authority over the enemy (Luke 10:19). Therefore, I stand in that authority, **annihilating** and **setting ablaze** with the fire of the Holy Spirit, the satanic spirit of control and manipulation, which is the enemy of my peace. I **plead the blood of Jesus** over my heart and mind. Forgive me, Father, for the times I think I have control over my own life and teach me how to trust You. Teach me how to lay aside all my burdens and lean not on my understanding (Proverbs 3:5-6). I **decree** and **declare** upon my head is the helmet of salvation (Ephesians 6:17). I will not conform to the patterns and ways of the world, but instead, I choose to renew my mind in Your Word (Romans 12:2). I choose to hope in You, Lord and to think upon those things that are true, honest, pure, lovely, and of good report. I **uproot**, **shatter**, and **reject** every lie of the enemy I have believed about myself and declare and decree I am free indeed. The lies of the enemy no longer have power over me. I surrender my will, emotions, and desires to You, Lord, for Your Word says if I delight in You, You will give me the desires of my heart. I want my heart's desires to align with the good plans You have for me (Jeremiah 29:11), so I choose to be still, trust You, obey You, and surrender to You in all areas of my life. In Jesus' name, I **bind** backlash and retaliation. Thank You, God, for fighting my battles and being exalted in every situation in my life. In Jesus' name. Amen.

Day 2
I Am Consistent!
by Ashley Banks

"Be assured and understand that the trial and proving your faith bring out endurance, steadfastness, and patience. But let endurance and steadfastness and patience have full play and do a thorough work, so that you may be [people] perfectly and fully developed [with no defects], lacking in nothing" (James 1:3-4, AMPC).

"Alright, I got this! I've got my plan together to make sure I stay on track. My notebook and planner are all set. I've got different color pens and highlighters to keep me focused. I mean, I'm really ready for this! I'm going all the way this time!"

How many of us have had this train of thought? I'll raise both my hands before you even have a chance. Because that was me—that is still me. Now, please don't get me wrong. I'm a good notebook and planner lover, really all things organization to carry out a well—thought-out plan. But what happens when everything around you is in place, yet, your endurance isn't? My endurance (aka my consistency) has been my biggest struggle.

That's what I like to call the "die-off" reaction. Yeah, I started out intending to see my goal, but then I just let it fade away. Maybe not intentionally but the whispers of the enemy start to ease in little by little, lie by lie—until I look up and I'm no longer studying the Word daily. Instead, I've made up my mind the floor must be swept at that very moment. It seems small and simple, but it's the smallest distractions or "need-to-do" things that add up and throw us off course in areas we know the Lord requires consistent endurance.

Still, it takes faith to trust the Lord will give you practical and personal instructions to carry out your consistency, becoming mature and healthy in His body. So, make the decision today to let it carry you out. Let your faith lead you to the instructions and your growing maturity lead you to obedience to carry out the steps the Lord has given. In your consistency and endurance, you will be perfected by the Perfecter of your faith. Consistency and perseverance are *required* to be fully developed and lacking nothing. Your Father God will use that growing endurance to move mountains, crush demons, break bloodline curses, and so much more—one moment, one decision, one God-given practical step at a time.

Reflection Exercise

Identify one area you know you've been inconsistent in, which you know God has called you to overcome. Be quiet before the Lord and ask Him, in faith, to provide you with personal and practical instructions to execute consistency in this area. Write down what God says to you (examples: setting daily phone reminders, getting an accountability partner, etc.). Then, declare, "I am consistent!" and thank Him for seeing you through to being fully developed and lacking nothing because it is so! You are consistent!

Warfare Prayer

Father God, right now, in the name of Jesus, I stand in the authority You have given me over everything that exalts itself against the knowledge of who You are. I **overthrow** and fully **annihilate** inconsistency in my life! Lord Jesus, Your living Word says faith without works is dead. I decree and declare I will be diligent for every work I commit to in faith because my faith is alive and well. In Jesus' name! You have given me the authority to **crush** and **tread on** all the powers of the enemy, and nothing will hurt me. So I hold firm to that, and I **crush** the enemy's attempts at making me feel weary. I will not grow weary in doing good because You promised a harvest in Your perfect timing when I do not give up. So, I will press on in endurance! I **bind** each plot, plan, and ploy of the enemy that would have me believe consistency is out of reach for me. Your Word says steadfastness will have its full effect. I release steadfastness right now. In the name of Jesus, that I may be perfect and complete, lacking nothing. I **pull down** the strongholds that have contributed to the past of inconsistency in my life with the mighty and never carnal weapons in You, Lord. I pull down the strongholds of fear, procrastination, lack of motivation, low energy, and laziness. In their places, I call forth the things that are not as though they are. I am motivated. I am energetic. I am a hard worker. I do everything in a timely fashion. I am confident. I am diligent, and I am consistent in every area of my life! I will pray until I see it and when I see it, I will protect it. I bind all backlash and retaliation. It is so! I am consistent! In Jesus' name. Amen.

Day 3
Are You Overwhelmed?
by Marci Bond

"Come to Me, all you who labor and are heavy-laden *and* overburdened, and I will cause you to rest. [I will ease and relieve and refresh your souls.]" (Matthew 11:28, AMPC).

As women, we tend to hold so many titles and oversee so many areas all at once. We all have professional and personal obligations. It is true we tend to hold multiple titles, take on numerous commitments, and manage many responsibilities all at once. We tend to give a lot of attention to our personal goals, business plans, academic and professional obligations, and invest time being concerned about our marriage relationship, as well as our other personal relationships. We also desire to maintain close friendships and try to spend time nurturing that area of our lives as well. As we oversee these areas and many more, we find ourselves taking on additional responsibilities. It is a given that at times we may be overwhelmed. Yet, society teaches us we are powerful women because we do so. However, we were never meant to operate in any role without the headship of our God and Father.

I have worn each of the hats I am describing. A time or two, I have found myself feeling drained, disconnected, personally neglected, and overwhelmed. There was a time in my career when I received lots of accolades from senior-level executives for my contribution to our corporate initiatives. I was repeatedly recognized for my administrative expertise. While I was receiving promotions and repeated salary upgrades, I was also a full-time college student, coordinating multiple events, and planning my wedding. Each area of obligation meant I carried an additional title. While I managed everything well many days, I must be honest and say the weight of it all was taxing. Not to mention, each obligation took time from my intimate relationship with God. Personally, when I find myself fighting to spend time with God, I know something is out of alignment, and I recognize this is the initial sign to reassess my priorities. I intentionally set aside time to seek God for His direction regarding each of my obligations. God showed me I was in a season of advancement. Yet, not every responsibility I assumed was in line with His will. Therefore, I had to surrender some responsibilities and rest in His divine wisdom.

*While God desires that we prosper in everything we do, we were never called to do any of it without Him and His leading.

I'd taken on so much I was literally out of God's presence and had to turn back to Him deliberately. When we are out of the presence of God, we are out of the will of God. The Oxford dictionary defines the word "overwhelmed" as 1) defeat completely, and 2) to give too much of a thing to someone; inundate. In other words, feeling overwhelmed is an assignment of the enemy to cause defeat, burden, and a lack of peace. But let us not overlook that it is also a cunning assignment to cause us to give too much time, energy, or focus to someone or something that inundates (takes over). If you sense you are feeling upset, burdened, or disconnected from God as a result of all you are doing, take the time to refocus and reestablish your priorities and rest in God. As you begin to rest in God, refocus and prioritize proper expectations for the many responsibilities you are managing. Prayerfully ask God what He wants you to do. Where am I out of alignment? God will light your path and give you rest.

Reflection Questions

1. What obligations are causing you anxiety, fear, or an overwhelming sense of concern?
2. What actions are you going to take to address feeling overwhelmed?

Warfare Prayer

Father, I thank You for peace in each role and assignment given to me. The thief comes only to steal, kill, and destroy. You came that we may have life and have it more abundantly (John 10:10). Therefore, I **abolish** every enemy's assignment to rob me of joy and peace in my assignment as a wife, mother, businesswoman, leader, student, etc. I **drive out** every demonic attack sent to cause defeat, burden, and a lack of peace in the divine assignments given to me. I **reject** the demonic assignment sent to separate me from You, Father God. Now, I cast all my cares upon You, declaring You care for me (1 Peter 5:7). I trust my life in Your hands and command I manage each assignment well, listen to the Holy Spirit, and follow the directions given to me. I declare I have complete peace, abundant life, and the fullness of joy as I carry out each assignment and title given to me. Lord, I trust You to lead me, and I yield every assignment to Your perfect counsel. I decree and declare You strengthen me. You help me, and You uphold me with Your righteous right hand (Isaiah 41:10). Mighty God, I thank You for taking away the burden from each assignment and giving me rest and relief. Thank You, Father God. It is in Jesus' name I seal this prayer, and I bind backlash and retaliation. In Jesus' name. Amen!

Day 4
The Trailblazer Anointing--You Are the First!
by Sukaena Callander

"We are assured and know that [God being a partner in their labor] all things work together and are [fitting into a plan] for good to and for those who love God and are called according to [His] design and purpose" (Romans 8:28 AMPC).

Have you ever felt as if everything around you was caving in and nothing you do can stop this sinking feeling? Well, that was me a year ago. I had enjoyed what I call a golden year of restoration in my marriage, which ended in a fantastic family holiday to Orlando. A trip to America from London with five children and my beloved husband was a blessing I truly appreciate God for allowing to happen.

Then, all of the sudden, my eldest son became exceptionally sleepy during this holiday. His neck was still very enlarged from what I thought was a sports injury six months before. He had to undergo some tests; two months later, he was diagnosed with stage four cancer. Three weeks later, my second and third sons were expelled from school, then lockdown began. I was overwhelmed and exhausted. However, during a one-to-one session with my mentor, I was reminded that God knows the challenges I was facing, since I told God "Yes!", He still expected me to fulfill the assignment He gave me while I am here on Earth.

Today, I am an author, a trainer for a range of training programs, host of a weekly motivational show, an intercessor called to the nations, and a budding entrepreneur. However, at that time, I was wallowing in self-pity and using my children as an excuse. Some may think I had a reason because I was already behind; my book should have been out a while ago. But it was delayed because I was distracted by my marital issues. I then launched into restoration, and my mentor gave me a lot of slack, but when I began to miss deadlines and kept using my circumstances as an excuse, I was pulled up in love by her. Yes, it hurt; yes, it was extremely uncomfortable, and yes, I just wanted to give up. One of my excuses was that I had no help, no example to follow. My mentor said, "Maybe the reason you don't have anyone to follow is that you are the first," Whew! It hit me! I went to the Holy Spirit, and while I moaned, I heard "crickets." Holy Spirit was quiet because He had already told me I was chosen. However, when I asked Holy Spirit again if I was the first, He said yes.

Two weeks after this breakthrough moment with God, I had a meeting. My mentor set a meeting with a few other mentees who I would describe as a bit behind, and it was then I received the download for my show—Sukey Saturdays was born! I set a date for the next week and launched.

I haven't looked back since. I was initially offended but only momentarily. I took the pull back. My mentor's name is Yvette, and it means archer. Yvette literally pulled me back to propel me forward. The same person who pulled me back is the same person advancing me by allowing me to train, teach, and let my God-given gifts flourish. I pressed into Christ, asking for more grace and discipline. I wrote my book during my son's treatment and just as he received his healing and the all-clear eight months after his initial diagnosis, I completed my first draft. The Lord told me to use this time to write and take my mind off my son's situation because he is healed. A year since my son's diagnosis, I have now completed and published my book, trained other women of God, written and delivered two of my own training programs, and published a journal.

I truly recognize God is my helper and if I am a chosen one, He will make a way, which He did. He provided financial and scriptural support. However, He showed me if I trusted Him, He would move me forward. During a recent training session, I was propelled by the same mentor who pulled me back. I heard the Lord say," Trailblazer anointing! You are the first!" When you don't have an example or a method to do something—your method, your coping mechanism, or how you overcome will be the example or role model for others to follow. That's what happened to me; my pull back was my propeller. I was last. I overcame offense, heard the Holy Spirit, prayed for more grace, and got into position. I was the last, but I'm now a leader by God's grace!

Reflection Exercise

1. Write a sentence about each area where you are behind, struggling, or feel overwhelmed in life.
2. Find scriptures that will help encourage you to get on track, for example,
   Psalm 25:15-22:

I look to the LORD for help at all times, and he rescues me from danger. Turn to me, LORD, and be merciful to me because I am lonely and weak. Relieve me of my worries and save me from all my troubles. Consider my distress and suffering and forgive all my sins. See how many enemies I have; see how much they hate me. Protect me and save me; keep me from defeat. I come to you for safety. May my goodness and honesty preserve me because I trust in you. From all their troubles, O God, save your people Israel!

Warfare Prayer

Lord, I **take authority** over every spirit of delay. As written in Psalms 25:15-16, "I look to the LORD for help at all times, and he rescues me from danger. Turn to me, LORD, and be merciful to me, because I am lonely and weak. Relieve me of my worries and save me from all my troubles." I **attack** the Destiny stealer, and I **thwart** every plan of the enemy. I **disallow** every hindering spirit that wants to destroy my destiny, dreams, and purpose. I **loose** the trailblazer anointing and declare that I will finish strong in all of our assignments. I declare and decree that the trailblazer anointing manifests in my life, my King's life and our children's lives. Father, propel me and give me the necessary discipline, self-control and humility to maintain my position so You alone get all the glory. As Your Word says in Psalm 25:21, "Protect me and save me; keep me from defeat. I come to you for safety. May your goodness and honesty preserve me because I trust in you."

I **cover** this prayer with the blood of Jesus, and I **cancel** any form of backlash or retaliation. In Jesus' matchless name we pray, Amen and Amen.

Day 5
Daddy's Girl
by Stephanie Canton

"Before I formed you in the womb I knew [and] approved of you [as My chosen instrument], and before you were born I separated and set you apart, consecrating you; [and] I appointed you to the nations" (Jeremiah 1:5, AMPC).

Are you familiar with the term "Daddy's girl"? Well, that is precisely who I was growing up. No matter what was going on in my little world, my daddy would make it alright. My father and I were incredibly close growing up. Although he and my mother split when I was very young, he remained very active in my life. He would attend school functions, pick me up on weekends, have surprise lunches with me, and of course, I was spoiled rotten. My daddy was "the man" in my eyes. Now granted, his lifestyle wasn't the best, and I was exposed more to life than I should've been as a child, but he was a great father to me.

I was about eight or nine years old and it was Easter Sunday—a big deal. Easter Sunday was one of the biggest holidays to celebrate. After all, it is the celebration of Jesus' resurrection. However, at eight or nine years of age, Easter for me meant getting all dressed up in a pretty dress, having my hair done and wearing it loosely, hanging down like a "big girl." Wearing my hair in any other style besides ponytails was a big deal to me back then. So here it was, Easter Sunday. I had on my pretty dress; my hair was freshly done, and I had some curls in it this year. I thought I was so beautiful, and I couldn't wait to show my daddy. I sat patiently in the living room. I was very careful not to wrinkle my dress. I heard my dad coming down the hall in his church shoes and as soon as I saw him, I jumped up in excitement, ran over to him, and said, "Daddy, how do I look?" His response was, "Pretty...darn (wasn't his choice word) ugly." Then he laughed and said, "Daddy is just joking; you are beautiful!"

Unfortunately, the damage was already done. I just didn't know the depths of it. At that moment, as quickly as I felt validated, was as quickly as I felt humiliated. Here I was at eight or nine. I had on a dress that others said was ugly. I wanted my hair fixed a certain way that others thought was ugly, but in my mind, I just knew my daddy would love it. It turned out my daddy thought what everyone else thought—that I was ugly. For the rest of my life up until around my twenties, receiving compliments was laughable. Whenever someone complimented me, I would always think, "yeah, right." Sometimes, I would look at the person as if the compliment had a pause, "You're beautiful...but." There were no buts, but that moment in my past never left me.

The enemy used a joke to try to ruin my identity. For a long time, a joke was my reality. No matter what I did, I never felt pretty enough, smart enough, or good enough! I remember I had just found out I was pregnant, and man, I thought my world was over. Here I was, a big disappointment yet again. After all, I had my child out of wedlock, and that was frowned upon. I remember crying so much and feeling so bad about everything. Every decision was a regret. I was really feeling "pretty darn ugly." I remember God whispering to me, "I still choose you." "I still called you." "You still belong to me." To be honest, I cried even harder when I heard that because I couldn't believe anybody would still want me. Yet, here it is the King of kings, Lord of lords, the Maker of it all, still chose me. After hearing from God, I had what I needed to be the mother I had to be.

You see, at that moment, God wanted me to know who I belonged to. That was the first revelation of my identity. Later in life, in my mid to late twenties, I remember my pastor telling me I had a calling on my life to preach, and I knew it was true. However, my past wasn't so pretty, so I really didn't think I had any business standing in anyone's pulpit to lead and guide them. I remember telling her I would think about whether or not I was the one truly qualified to give a trial sermon given my past transgressions. While I was studying, God gave me the scripture Jeremiah 1:5, "Before I formed you in the womb, I knew you, and before you were born, I consecrated you; I have appointed you as a prophet to the nations." Now, not only do I know who I am, I also know whose I am—my Daddy's girl!

Reflection Questions

1. Who does God say you are?

2. Did you know who God says you are outranks everyone else's opinion of you?

Warfare Prayer

In the name of Jesus, Father God, I come in the authority You have given me to **bomb** the spirit of false identity. Your Word says, "Before I formed you in the womb I knew you, and before you were born I consecrated you; I have appointed you as a prophet to the nations" (Jeremiah 1:5). Your Word tells us, "For we are God's handiwork, created in Christ Jesus to do good works, which God prepared in advance for us to do" (Ephesians 2:10). So, I decree and declare I am chosen to do Your excellent work. I **set ablaze** every thought that tries to penetrate my mind, and I decree I have the mind of Christ. I set my mind on things above and not earthly things as Your Word says in Colossians 3:2 I send Holy Ghost fire to **burn out** every word spoken over me to make me feel I am not pretty enough, smart enough, or bold enough to be who God has called me to be and to do what God has called me to do. Genesis 1:26 says I was created in Your image and likeness. Your Word says in Matthew 22:14 many are called, but few are chosen. I decree and declare I am chosen. I **nullify** and **cancel** every demonic assignment that has been sent to attack my identity. I know who I am and who I belong to. In the name of Jesus, I declare your Word that says I am more than a conqueror. I am the head and not the tail. I am above and not beneath. I cancel all backlash and retaliation. In Jesus' name. Amen.

Day 6
What If It Actually Works?
by Giovan Clifton

But now, this is what the Lord, your Creator says, O Jacob, And He who formed you, O Israel, "Do not fear, for I have redeemed you [from captivity]; I have called you by name; you are Mine! When you pass through the waters, I will be with you; And through the rivers, they will not overwhelm you. When you walk through fire, you will not be scorched, nor will the flame burn you. For I am the Lord your God, The Holy One of Israel, your Savior; I have given Egypt [to the Babylonians] as your ransom, Cush (ancient Ethiopia) and Seba [its province] in exchange for you. Because you are precious in My sight, You are honored, and I love you, I will give other men in return for you and other peoples in exchange for your life. (Isaiah 43:1-4, AMPC)

It was the summer of 2011. I was in my mid-twenties with several failed businesses under my belt. I guess you could call me a serial entrepreneur. My father believed in me and invested $10,000 for me to start yet another adventure: a bounce house company! I had big dreams for this business. I knew I would have the largest bounce house company in Northwest Indiana. In my mind, I would have a warehouse with several bounce houses going out every day, a fleet of trucks, and a team of workers. In reality, I had a pacific, four bounce houses, and small children helping to load and unload the equipment. I prayed several times a day for God to increase my business, increase the demand, and send help. Daddy God did just that!

As my business began to grow, I had repeat customers and faithful workers. It was like a dream come true, but I had actually seen this play out several times. In my mind, I knew I wanted to be successful, but in my heart, there was fear and failure because of condemnation. My core was tainted and filled with insecurities I didn't know existed until my ventures came to screeching halts. I was afraid I wasn't good enough. I thought I wasn't qualified. I was scared of success, so I quit before the business could "disappoint me." This mindset spilled over into other areas of my life, like my relationships. I had to change how I saw myself and trust Daddy God with my entire life.

I had placed all my faith in myself, and that's why I failed every time. I had to put my faith in Christ Jesus. I had to use the Word of God and take my thoughts captive because, in Him, I have been made righteous. This guarantees that I have one hundred percent victory, one hundred percent of the time. There is no failure in Him, so there is no failure in me. I began to see myself as victorious both inside and out, and I now have thriving businesses and thriving relationships. He has given me the victory!

Reflection Question

To what degree does fear and condemnation keep you from success?

Warfare Prayer

Heavenly Father, I thank You for giving me victory over the enemy. You said the enemies that revolt against me will be defeated before my face (Deuteronomy 28: 7). Therefore, I **destroy** every assignment of hell against my life that would try to alter my destiny. I decree and declare no fear in me but power, love, and a sound mind (2 Timothy 1:7). I will not fear because Jesus Christ redeemed me (Isaiah 43:1). The Word of God says, "The Lord my God wins victory after victory and is always with me. He celebrates and sings because of me, and he will refresh my life with his love" (Zephaniah 3:17, CEVDCI). Therefore, I **take authority** over every spirit that will try to cause me to retreat. I **smother** you out now. In the name of Jesus! I will not turn back, but I will finish strong. I **slice** every thought of condemnation. I loose shame upon the enemy's camp! I think of things that are pure, lovely, and praiseworthy (Philippians 4: 8). I have a finisher's anointing! I am successful! I am from God. I have overcome the world (1 John 5: 4). I **cancel** backlash and retaliation! In Jesus' name. Amen!

Day 7
Sharing Is Beautiful
by Anja Collins

"And they have overcome (conquered) him by means of the blood of the Lamb and by the utterance of their testimony, for they did not love and cling to life even when faced with death [holding their lives cheap till they had to die for their witnessing]" (Revelation 12:11, AMPC)

I was in elementary school the first time someone called me an old lady. I do not remember who said it, but I know there was a general consensus that Anja was more "mature" than everyone else. To me, that meant I was "different." Several things set me apart. For starters, I had to repeat the first grade when I switched schools, so this made me the oldest in my class. I was the largest and most deeply melanated girl. I was animated, loud, and liked to talk a lot, so this kept me in the hot seat. I had a deep love for smooth jazz and classical music at the age of 7. Also, I liked really, really expensive things. Adults made comments about my tastes and made me feel as if something was wrong with me. Thus, a root of shame and hiding sprung forth.

My grandmother, who introduced my love of fine experiences, passed away when I was 7. I believe she would have been a comrade and source of support against the world had she lived. Unfortunately, I was left with a lot of people who just did not understand me. People indulged me—but they did not understand.

So, I hid my gifts and kept my talents to myself. I only shared aspects of me with those whom I wanted. As I grew older, I enjoyed the secrecy and the mysterious allure that I had. I developed an arrogant attitude too. When others would share with me some new thing they experienced, I would smirk—"been there, done that." There goes a spirit of pride to accompany the shame.

Until God started nudging me to share. That little girl started rearing her head. Oh no! Share with whom, Lord? Not those who laughed at me and called me a rich, old woman. Let them figure it out!

The enemy meant for the hurt little girl to be suppressed and stop dreaming, sharing, and expecting greater. That technically didn't happen because the measure of faith given to me was a gift from God. But, for a long time, the enemy perverted the purpose of that gift. Instead of encouraging and urging me, I was dodging and hiding.

The Lord's remedy for me has been to share. Share in the form of writing, pictures and documentation. Share how beautiful He is, how grand He is, how big He wants us to dream so we can put our current circumstances into perspective. Sharing my life, the love I have, and the things I experience allows others to see God's expression of beauty through me, setting the little girl who was told she thinks way too grand free!

What's interesting is those kids who made fun of me are now adults. And their palates have changed. As we share, it's a beautiful thing.

Reflection Questions

1. What gifts, talents, and personality quirks made you unique as a child?
2. Have you used these gifts to your advantage?

46

Warfare Prayer

In the mighty name of Jesus Christ, I **shut down** the demonic assignments of shame and hiding. I decree and declare that now is the time I will let my light shine. Lord, Your Word says we have been fearfully and wonderfully made and so marvelous are Your works (Psalm 139:14). Therefore, I will no longer hide or cover the gifts, talents, and creative abilities You planted in me at birth. I **uproot** all selfishness within every facet of my being, and I share (Hebrews 13:16). As I share, I am being set free. The more I share, the freer I become! Your Word says whom the Son has set free is free indeed (John 8:36), and I declare I am free! I **cancel** all backlash and retaliation and seal this prayer in the blood of Jesus. Amen.

Day 8
Deliverance of Her Womb
by Khatarrie Durden

"He said to them, Because of the littleness of your faith [that is, your lack of firmly relying on trust]. For truly I say to you, if you have faith [that is living] like a grain of mustard seed, you can say to this mountain, move from here to yonder place, and it will move; and nothing will be impossible to you" (Matthew 17:20, AMPC).

Do you understand nothing is impossible for the only living God? I understood this going into my second pregnancy because I knew spiritual warfare this time. I knew in my spirit things were going to be different. I understood the power of life and death was in my tongue, so I made sure to be extra careful with the things I allowed people to speak over me and what I let come out of my mouth. With my first pregnancy, I was diagnosed with a condition called incompetent cervix, which is no longer valid because of the healing blood of Jesus. I was admitted to the hospital for eight weeks with my first pregnancy, and doctors told my husband and me I would most likely miscarry, and we would lose our son, but God said differently. While in the hospital, I studied the Word of God more than I have ever done in my entire life. I prayed harder than I have ever had to, and all glory to God, I birthed a beautiful baby boy who was born at 32 weeks. He had to stay in the NICU (newborn intensive care unit) for about four weeks, but I was able to bring him home completely healthy. He is now the most joyful, energetic toddler you could ever meet!

FAST FORWARD to my second pregnancy, I knew this time would be different. I was spiritually more mature and understood my authority in Jesus Christ. I declared healing over my womb every night, and I said my confidence rested in my healer and protector. I prayed that my husband, children, and I would be protected throughout my entire pregnancy and childbirth. I declared I would not worry or be afraid because the Lord, my God, fights for me, which comforted me more than anything. Remembering my Abba Daddy has already won the battle brought me the ultimate peace. I declared my children are perfectly healthy in the name of Jesus. I declared my household will serve the Lord. I declared my medical care team would receive counsel from the Lord and have my best interest at heart. Finally, I canceled all assignments sent from the enemy against my husband, marriage, children, and our lives. I declared there would be no backlash or retaliation in the name of Jesus. I paired it with Scripture as we are taught in the Helpmeet Army. I put myself on the battlefield like David, in front of everyone, broadcasting the work God was going to do in my pregnancy and labor. My weapon was the sword of the Spirit, which is the Word of God. It has never failed me yet. By applying the Word of God to my life, I was able to watch it come alive before my eyes. My beautiful, healthy baby girl was born at home with no medical complications. I allowed God to get all the glory by putting myself out there to prove to others He is worthy! Now, I do not know what you may be struggling with, but I beg of you today to step out on that battlefield with the only true, living King and fight. You will not be disappointed.

Reflection Question

Take some time to think about your life. What are some of the biggest challenges (mountains) you are facing right now? Find three or more scriptures that contradict the problem you are currently facing. Declare these scriptures over your problems while in prayer. Remember according to the Word of God, we have what we say.

Warfare Prayer

I decree and declare the mountains weighing me down will be moved. In the name of Jesus! It is written if we have faith even as small as a mustard seed, we can say to the mountain to move from here to there, and it will move (Matthew 17:20)! In the mighty name of Jesus, I **annihilate** all doubt trying to hinder my belief, and I speak that I have steadfast faith. Lord, I declare You are my refuge and strong tower against the enemy! (Psalms 61:3) I **tear down** all assignments meant to distract me! I will move by faith and not by sight (2 Corinthians 5:7). Therefore, I will not be moved by my circumstances, but I will pray to God, for nothing is impossible for the Lord. I bind backlash and retaliation. In Jesus' name. Amen!

Day 9
Hope for the Hurting
by Mary Elam

"May the God of your hope so fill you with all joy and peace in believing [through the experience of your faith] that by the power of the Holy Spirit you may abound and be overflowing (bubbling over) with hope" (Romans 15:13 AMPC).

Have you ever been in such pain there seemed to be no end? You have cried on your pillow until it was completely soaked with your tears. God sees, and He knows. His love for you is never-ending. He desires to heal your pain. Come to Him. Matthew 11:28 says, "Come to me all who labor and are heavy laden, and I will give you rest. Take my yoke upon you, and learn of me, for I am gentle and lowly in heart, and you will find rest for your souls. For my yoke is easy, and my burden is light." God is saying, give Me your struggles and pain, and I will provide you with Me. He wants you to exchange your pain for His strength. He wants to do life with you. He desires to commune with you and teach you how to relinquish your struggles and grow in Him.

Does this mean you will no longer have pain? No, but the Creator of the universe wants to give you the strength and power, not only to endure but also to enjoy the journey. Yes, you can have joy in the midst of pain. I have encountered such pain in my life I felt I would never get out of my bed. The pain was so crushing I just wanted to sleep my life away, but God continued to pursue me in the midst of my pain. I cried out to my God, and He strengthened me with each new day. Although there was no change in my circumstances, He showed me He alone was my joy. I read the Word and stood on His promises. 1 Peter 5:7 instructs us to "Cast your cares upon Him for He cares for You." I laid my burdens at His feet, and I continued to see His glory in my life. His Word is so accurate. His Word was my lifeline. As I went deeper into His Word and cried out to Him in prayer, I began to see changes in me.

You see, change begins with us first. As I changed, I saw my circumstances differently. God began to teach me how to pray and intercede. I was no longer a victim, but I became a warrior for the mighty King of kings. I found my purpose in the midst of my pain. Our heavenly Papa desires your heart. He wants to use you for His glory. Give Him your pain and allow Him to give you His joy, love, and peace. It is yours for the asking.

Reflection Question

The King of Glory instructs us to lay our pain at His feet, and He will give us hope. What are 3–5 actions you can take to strengthen your hope?

Warfare Prayer

Father, I give You glory. I bless You for always being there, even in the midst of my pain. Lord, I **crush** and **annihilate** the spirit of discouragement and hopelessness. You are the God of more than enough, You are my hope restorer. Your Word declares in Jeremiah 29:11, "'For I know the plans I have for you,' declares the Lord, 'plans to prosper you and not to harm you, plans to give you hope and a future.'" I release peace, joy, and the love of the Father. I decree and declare the curse of hopelessness is **uprooted** from my heart. Isaiah 40:31 says, "But they who wait for the Lord shall renew their strength; they shall mount up with wings like eagles; they shall run and not be weary; they shall walk and not faint." Father, not only are You giving me my hope back, but You are also strengthening me for each new day. I am made fresh in You, and You have given me an overflow of benefits. I **bind** backlash and retaliation. In Jesus' name. Amen.

Day 10
Lay Down Your Life
by Michelle Engles

"Blessed (enjoying enviable happiness, spiritually prosperous—with life-joy and satisfaction in God's favor and salvation, regardless of their outward conditions) are the makers *and* maintainers of peace, for they shall be called the sons of God!" (Matthew 5:9, AMPC)

The first words I ever heard from the Lord and knew without a shadow of a doubt were from Him were "Be still." Somewhat early on, while my husband and I were separated, it became apparent that even in his wayward lifestyle, my husband was seeking peace. I knew it was due to the spiritual battle raging within him as both the enemy and God were fighting for his destiny and purpose. However, I couldn't even begin to get the peace he needed until I could lay my husband, marriage, and life on the altar. I had to learn to be still and trust the same God who created the heavens and the earth could make beauty from the ashes of my marriage. To do that, I first had to find my own inner healing. The spiritual healing I found in the Lord allowed my emotional healing to occur. As I healed, I found the peace my husband needed. My spiritual eyes were opened to see the truth about who my husband was and the situation I was in. As my faith grew, I said to God, "Even if You don't, I will still follow where You lead because I know Your ways are higher and better than anything I could ever think or imagine." This could only happen when I allowed the Prince of Peace to invade and take over my life.

And now, as my marriage is being reconciled and restored, God keeps reminding me how vital peace within our household is. As a homeschool mom with three boys and multiple businesses my husband and I own, life can easily get chaotic. God is continually reminding me He needs me to find ways to create peace within our household. For me, that means staying ahead of the chaos as much as possible and trying my best to be prepared for all things. This means knowing the past tactics the enemy has used against me, my husband, marriage, and family. It also means being proactive and doing things like anointing my home, declaring the peace of God, and placing the whole armor of God upon me and my family daily.

Peace is a daily decision. We can decide to let the chaos of life and the world create unrest and division within our marriages and lives, or we can remind ourselves God is not the author of confusion. Peace encompasses so many of the attributes of God; healing, forgiveness, and love are a few. However, these must first reside within you. God's blessings in your life can abound once you allow yourself to be a maker and maintainer of His peace.

I now understand the words "Be still" that God had spoken to me at the beginning of my storm. In the stillness, I was able to hear His continued instruction. In the stillness, I was able to heal. In the stillness, I was able to love. In the stillness, I was able to receive and be a vessel for the peace that surpasses all understanding.

Reflection Questions

1. What things can you do to create peace in your life, marriage, and family?

2. What currently prevents you from allowing peace to enter your life and be the peacemaker God has called you to be?

Warfare Prayer

In the name of Jesus, Father God, I **annihilate** all fear and anxiety residing within my heart and mind. I **uproot** all bitterness, hurt, and anger within me and release Your healing blood over my life. I declare I will no longer allow the enemy to use me to create chaos. I am a child of the Most High God (Galatians 3:26-29), and I lay my life down as a living sacrifice to the purposes of Your kingdom (Romans 12:1). I place the shoes of the preparation of the gospel of peace upon my feet (Ephesians 6:15), knowing I always have You as my firm foundation in all things (2 Timothy 2:19). I **take authority** over every situation in my life, marriage, and family that is creating unrest and disunity. You, Lord, are a God of unity and order (1 Peter 3:8; 1 Corinthians 14:33), and I release those over my life and situation now. I declare I am the bloodline breaker. Chaos, quarreling, and unrest are permanently cut off from my generational line. As I allow myself to be a vessel of Your peace, I declare Your blessings over my life and family now and for at least a thousand generations to follow (Deuteronomy 7:9). I **cancel** backlash and retaliation. In the mighty name of Jesus Christ! Amen!

Day 11
Swimming in Deep Waters
by Dr. Katrina Foster

"When you pass through the [deep] waters, I will be with you, and through the rivers, they will not overwhelm you. When you walk through the fire, you will not be burned or scorched, nor will the flame kindle upon you" (Isaiah 43:2, AMPC).

I grew up with the misapprehension that Black people don't swim. When I was young, I was told swimming would mess up my hair, and it would be hard to untangle. As I got older, I was told many of my ancestors drowned when they jumped off the slave ship after being captured, so they wouldn't suffer any more bondage and captivity. In short, it was ingrained in me that swimming could not be a source of enjoyment and entertainment for Black people. These reasons made logical sense to me, so I never tried to learn how to swim. I may have stood in the shallow end of a pool, but I refused to put my head underwater. I refused until I went to college and found out I had to either take a swim test or learn to swim to pass PE class. I voiced my anger and frustration to the instructor asking for an exemption from completing this task, but she didn't budge. However, over time (and my tears), her gentleness and patience gave me the confidence I needed to learn how to hold my breath, float, and finally, how to swim.

In retrospect, I learned so much more from that experience beyond the mechanics of swimming. For one, I realized once you know how to swim, the depth of the pool doesn't matter. The size of the pool in and of itself cannot prevent someone from being able to get through it and make it to dry land. Similarly, I learned the notion that deep waters have the power in and of itself to overtake me was also a misapprehension. These lessons apply to me in the spiritual sense as well. Right now, I am metaphorically wading through a large body of deep waters physically, emotionally, mentally, and financially. I have a whole list: setbacks, doubts, disappointments, despair, discouragement, delays, loss, trauma, frustration, chronic health conditions, and heartbreak that could cause me to drown.

Even Jesus experienced the weight of sadness and pain that comes when someone is suffering in deep waters. He knew He was about to be crucified to atone for all of our sins while in the Garden of Gethsemane. I can only imagine how scared, frustrated, and angry He must have felt. Nevertheless, He said, "Father, if you are willing, please take this cup of suffering away from me. Yet I want your will to be done, not mine" (Luke 22:42). Desiring God's perfect will to be done above and beyond your worries, doubts, and fears is the difference-maker. As Pastor Steven Furtick said, "What you see is no match for what God has spoken." Through studying, speaking, and submerging myself in God's Word, He gently and patiently reminds me I can get through deep waters—not because of me in and of myself, but I've learned to tap into His supernatural power and strength to keep going, believing one day, I will experience the goodness of the Lord in the land of the living.

Because of Him, I can keep swimming in deep waters.

Reflection Exercise

List three challenges—your deep waters. Next to each challenge, write a scripture that contains God's specific promise to you regarding that challenge.

Warfare Prayer

I declare God uses my suffering for His glory. His power is made perfect in my weakness. He uses my challenges to accomplish His perfect purpose for my life. I **set ablaze** the spirit of disgrace upon my life and legacy. Holy Spirit, help me **take captive** every thought that tries to exalt itself above the knowledge of You, God (2 Corinthians 10:5). Your Word says I have the authority to **trample** on snakes and scorpions and overcome all the enemy's power; nothing will harm me (Luke 10:19). I **bomb** anxiety. I am not anxious about anything, but in everything, I present my requests to You, God, through prayer and petition with thanksgiving. And Your peace, which transcends all understanding, guards my heart and my mind in Christ Jesus (Philippians 4:6-7). I am encouraged by the Word of God to keep going, for the Bible says, "When the righteous cry for help, the Lord hears and delivers them out of all their troubles. The Lord is near to the brokenhearted and saves the crushed in spirit. Many are the afflictions of the righteous, but the Lord delivers him out of them all. He keeps all his bones; not one of them is broken" (Psalm 34:17-20). I take up the shield of faith with which I **extinguish** all the flaming arrows of the evil one (Ephesians 6:16). I declare I trust You, God, too much to give up. In Jesus' name. Amen. I **cancel** all backlash and retaliation. In the name of Jesus. Amen.

Day 12
How to Go Through - Journey to the Breakthrough
by Hyasmin Harper

"Have I not commanded you? Be strong, vigorous, and very courageous. Be not afraid, neither be dismayed, for the Lord your God is with you wherever you go" (Joshua 1:9, AMPC).

Six months before the beginning of a season, something happened in my life that would test my faith to the brink of life or death mentally, emotionally, physically, and spiritually. I received a prophetic call that said, "All your dreams will come to pass, but you have to go through." That's all my brother in Christ said as he followed the prompting of the Holy Spirit. Then I received a text from a sister in Christ that said, "God is doing something mighty in your husband! A mighty breakthrough!"

After that, the storm started. My 13-year marriage went down, crumbling uncontrollably in one day. I had no time to understand. I fasted for 21 days, and God said, "Submit to everything your husband is about to instruct you." He said we needed to sell the house now, and then he would file for divorce. All I held onto was "This is a breakthrough," and I must go through it. In three months, the house was sold. A $300K equity profitable house ended in a $30K profit; divorce never occurred. I asked God, "Can you please just give me something to hold on to?" God prophetically showed me the cross. I sensed Him say, "There are two roads: the right and the left. Whatever you and your husband choose leads to death (death to self). No matter what both of you decide, I will never leave or forsake you (Deuteronomy 31:6).

I ended up in a one-bedroom apartment—separated. I tried to control my outcome. The first road I took was the world's way. I hired a coach who had gone through what I went through, but her outcome was divorce and a happy new marriage with a new husband. I aspired to that, so I hired her. God had humor. In my first session, she said, "Do you want to heal fast? Forgive!" God used her to soften my heart instantly. I wanted to heal, control my outcome, and move on. I sure did heal fast. I was ready to move on, but God said open the door of communication to your husband, pray for him and know I have healed you. He also said He would show me how to strengthen my husband (Galatians 6:1-3).

It has been a year and a half of separation. God showed me the promise from the beginning, but the journey has been a step-by-step process. As a person who has held the title of Financial Controller for over 15 years professionally, God took me on a journey of surrender—the journey to the deliverance of control! Also, in this season, my father passed, and I have a mother who has been battling cancer for nine years. To top it off, I had to overcome seven miscarriages. God made sure I was in a position of "out of control" for an opportunity to see His saving grace.

So how do you go through the seasons of life that are pressing you on every side? Be encouraged and know God is there every step of the way. Enjoy each moment, every single minute! Hours and days are precious. Surrender each day unto the Lord. Watch and see how your intimacy grows with Him daily.

My story is not done, and I do not focus on the promise in a fleshly manner anymore. I have now surrendered the promise to God. I have learned to find joy in the Lord each day. No matter the circumstance, knowing God is with me is what matters (James 1:2-4). I see how God is restoring in His way and His timing. I am content with that (2 Corinthians 12:9).

Reflection Question

When you are going through a season of various trials, what strategies do you use to get through it?

Warfare Prayer

Spirit of control, I serve you notice in the mighty name of Jesus. In the name of Jesus, I **bind** the spirit of control that keeps me in bondage and fear of tomorrow. In the mighty name of Jesus, I release peace, joy, and rest that the spirit of control has bound. You will bow down to His mighty name now! For it is written in 2 Timothy 1:7, "For God hath not given us the spirit of fear; but of power, and love, and of a sound mind." Satan, you have no control over me today or tomorrow, for it is written in Jeremiah 29:11 (The Message Bible), "I'll show up and take care of you as I promised and bring you back home. I know what I'm doing. I have it all planned out—plans to take care of you, not abandon you, plans to give you the future you hope for." So today, Lord, teach us to number our days as You said in Psalm 90:12. You are the timekeeper, so I rest in Your wings, my God of all my days. I **bind** all backlash and retaliation. In Jesus' mighty name. Amen.

Day 13
Unwinding
by Shalenie Hunter

"For we are God's [own] handiwork (His workmanship), recreated in Christ Jesus, [born anew] that we may do those good works which God predestined (planned beforehand) for us [taking paths which He prepared ahead of time], that we should walk in them [living the good life which He prearranged and made ready for us to live]" (Ephesians 2:10, AMPC).

Sometimes God will allow us to experience situations or circumstances to bring us to the end of ourselves (unwinding). In my case, it is what He has done. Being born and raised in a Christian household (a pastor's granddaughter) and my other grandparents were active members in the church), I've always felt blessed and highly favored. Though I didn't give my life to Christ until my late 20s, I've always thought I had a connection with God, and He has and will always bless me.

Growing up in a relatively large family (six sisters and one brother), I've seen how God's blessings were flowing in my life. One of my most significant examples of God's blessings/favor had to be about when I was seven years old, and I had a desire to learn to swim. I never had any means or idea how it would happen. However, fast forward to the age of thirteen. I migrated to the United States and God made the provision. I gained the opportunity to learn how to swim.

Again, we serve an awesome God. Not only did He provide the chance to learn, but He also went above and beyond. He placed people in my life who would encourage me and lead me to become captain of my school's swim team and gain employment as a lifeguard at sixteen. The favor was not just for me, but it was also for my entire family because I was able to help my parents ease some of the pressure of providing for eight children. As stated, that was one of the many examples of how God has always been faithful in my life.

Since giving my life to Christ, I developed a false identity of God and His requirements due to the many blessings bestowed on my life. So, let's go back to my topic, "Unwinding." A scripture that comes to mind is Luke 12:48; "But he that knew not and did commit things worthy of stripes, shall be beaten with few stripes. For unto whom much is given, of him shall be much required" (KJV). I thought coming to Christ meant all my problems would be easily fixed or even be obsolete. But if God blessed me so much before surrendering my life to Him, how much more will He do for me? I was so wrapped and tangled up in myself it was ridiculous. But for God's grace and mercy, He had to take me through a season of unwinding.

These past three and half years have been the most challenging years I've had to face in my life. Due to my lack of knowledge and false humility, I almost missed the mark on my journey with Christ. I've experienced some of those stripes Luke talked about in verse 48. I idolized the same blessings (my marriage and family) He gave me more than Him. I was living in a facade as a follower of Christ; however, I was nothing more than a lukewarm, pride-filled, deceived churchgoer claiming to be a Christ-follower. The enemy used my lack of knowledge and zeal for God to have a field day in my life.

I am so thankful to God that though I had to go through an unwinding process (attacks on my marriage and family), God is turning and will turn it all around for my good. Through coming to the end of myself (unwinding), I've learned what "the much" is that God expects of me. According to Ephesians 2:10, "For we are his workmanship, created in Christ Jesus unto good works, which God hath before ordained that we should walk in them." It is through true surrender that I began to take on God's true identity of me. In true humility, I had to let go of all the idols and false ideologies in my life that had me tangled and yield to God's unwinding. If you can relate to this devotion, submit to God; trust Him, and let Him unwind you today. Your life will never be the same.

Reflection Exercise

1. What are some things that might be keeping you tangled or wrapped up in self (stopping you from knowing what God's expectations are of you)?

2. List at least three strategies you can use to let God help you unwind to move/operate in the calling He has for you.

Warfare Prayer

Father, in the name of Jesus, I **come against** pride and false humility. I **crush**, **dismantle**, and **eradicate** the enemy's deception that he tries to use to keep us from walking in our true identity and purpose You have for us. Father, You said in Your Word we are Your workmanship, created in Christ Jesus unto good works, which You have before ordained for us to walk in (Ephesians 2:10). Therefore, I **trample** all the lies the enemy uses to tangle and wrap us up in ourselves. I **annihilate** every residue that blinds us and enables us to place idols above You, the Almighty God. I declare and decree we know the truth, and we are set free. We humble ourselves under the mighty hand of God and **renounce** the spirit of pride in our lives. We lay down our wills and ways for Yours. I release the fruit of humility over us, and we take on the image of Christ. I declare we are no longer tangled, wrapped up, or blinded by lies. We have the mind of Christ, and our thoughts and ways line up with Yours. We trust in You, Lord, with all our hearts and acknowledge You in all our ways. Thank You for making our paths straight. There will be no backlash or retaliation. In Jesus' name. Amen!

Day 14
Loving the Unlovable
by Janelle Hutcheson

"But God clearly shows *and* proves His own love for us, by the fact that while we were still sinners, Christ died for us" (Romans 5:8, AMPC).

Katharine Hepburn once said, "Love has nothing to do with what you are expecting to get, only with what you are expecting to give, which is everything." My life has been decorated with a mix of many interesting experiences. Perhaps you can relate to some or all of this one.

Most of my early years were filled with adventure, fun, and innocent freedom that children love and should enjoy. I had close friends who valued and appreciated me, and a church community that adopted, shielded, and poured into my life. My parents sacrificed to provide me with their best, and my family supported me no matter what. I felt loved. I was loved. My natural response was to love my parents, family, and friends because of how they treated me. In my eyes, they were "loveable."

Some of my adult experiences presented a stark contrast to my earlier years. The harsh reality of adult life, the choices made by others that affected me, misunderstandings and disagreements that strained some of my most intimate relationships were now my reality. The sting of betrayal, intentional or unintentional, from colleagues, friends, and even close family members hurt my feelings. I felt abused, taken advantage of, and underappreciated. It was no longer my natural response to love these people. In my eyes, they are "unlovable."

My initial natural response to the "unlovable" was resentment, dislike, disdain. It is hard to consider and even love people who seem not deserving of our time, attention, and love, if we are honest. We may consider forgiving those who hurt us but may think, do we really have to love those who spitefully use us? The more I mature in my walk with Christ, the more I realize and accept His ways are not our ways, and though He doesn't change, He is always calling us higher so we can go from glory to glory. If we utterly understand His nature and how His kingdom operates, maybe it will help us do and act as He requires.

Let's face it: society's norms usually contradict the spiritual beliefs and principles by which Christians should live. This shouldn't come as a surprise since, as believers, we aren't of this world (John 17:16). If our kingdom is from another world (John 18:36), we are in this world but not of it. Our primary kingdom is invisible, but the one we reside in is visible, albeit the invisible kingdom is more authentic (2 Corinthians 4:13). Yet, the visible kingdom seems to captivate our minds and influence our behavior more potently. According to our kingdom, this should not be so because we walk by faith and not by sight.

If I am transparent, my concept and perception of love was and has been heavily influenced by my experiences in this earthly kingdom. The day I got the revelation I was guilty of and at times "unlovable" is the day I began to see the "unlovable" as Christ saw them.

Our very redemption was wrought while we were yet "sinners" (Romans 5:8). God continues to choose to love us as nothing can separate us from His love (Romans 8:35).

I encourage you to take some time to meditate on what I find to be the most extraordinary love story ever told through any of the Gospels. The story of Jesus and His true submission to His Father and the love of His Father who gave His only Son for us is a blueprint of how we should live. Even though the theme of betrayal (Judas and Peter), isolation (praying alone with no one to agree with you before a pivotal life moment), hurt (people He healed and helped turn their backs on Him), disappointment (people were mean and heartless as He carried the cross) are evident, He still chose to give His life for all of the unlovable. He didn't rely on His feelings. Instead, He decided to love His Father still and love the unlovable (you and me).

Reflection Question

Since you are one of God's beloved children, what are some actions you can take to better model our King's example/kingdom behavior?

Warfare Prayer

In the name of Jesus, I **crush** the spirit of resentment, hate, and vengeance. I **sever** the spirit of retaliation. I **shred to pieces** all the lies the enemy has plagued me with regarding how You love me. I declare I have the power to grasp how wide and long and high and deep Your love is for me and to know this love that surpasses knowledge (Ephesians 3:17-19). Because Your love is sincere, I hate what is evil, and I cling to what is good (Romans 12:9). I am devoted to others in brotherly love (Romans 12:10), and I abide in love, so I do no harm to my neighbor (Romans 13:10). I walk in love (1 Corinthians Chapter 13), and I have the fruit of the Spirit, including love in Jesus' name. I **bind** all backlash and retaliation. In Jesus' name. Amen.

Day 15
Worship Is My Weapon
by Maxine Baker Jackson

Blessed be the God and Father of our Lord Jesus Christ, the Father of sympathy (pity and mercy) and the God [Who is the Source] of every comfort (consolation and encouragement), Who comforts (consoles and encourages) us in every trouble (calamity and affliction), so that we may also be able to comfort (console and encourage) those who are in any kind of trouble or distress, with the comfort (consolation and encouragement) with which we ourselves are comforted (consoled and encouraged) by God. (2 Corinthians 1:3-4, AMPC)

Many people would agree that 2020 was full of hardship, uncertainty, separation, civil unrest, and loss. It was effortless to focus on the negative, as negativity seemed to be all around us. If it wasn't personal, it was on our jobs, in our communities, widespread throughout our nation. We were all affected somehow. Being mindful of my physical, mental, and spiritual health was an assignment of overwhelming stress, even more so having to make those same considerations for my spouse, children, and an aging parent while confined to a quarantined space and limited resources. Ugh!

Deep breaths.

You are reading this, so that means you survived, along with me! However, I'm sure not without some scars, bruises, or injuries that still have a lingering effect today. And that is okay. You are fine. You are still here. I learned from that last season what I may have lost or stand in need of can be restored. I can be restored. When the enemy comes in like a flood, that's the time to stand your ground, put on your armor, and make ready your weapons.

My flood was becoming a homeschool teacher to my very active and zealous young children, supporting my children through the confusion and transition of the "new normal," protecting my family from a virus I knew nothing about, managing a household on limited resources, then on none after losing my job, being a rescue to a parent across the country who was unexpectedly hospitalized, losing not one but multiple family members in the less than a 6-month timeframe, sustaining two major car accidents only weeks apart, and all while being faithful to my mentoring group, my church home, the assignment God has for me in this earth. I was overwhelmed and pressured, and I wanted to give up. But the Father of mercies and God of comfort reminded me I was not alone. I was fully armed and equipped to handle this, and no weapon formed against me would prosper.

Once I stopped and refocused, I remembered my weapon of worship. Most of the time, people refer to worship as a slow song we sing before church service begins to set the atmosphere. Worship is so much more. My weapons of worship look like this: 1) prayer 2) fasting 3) singing/praising 4) yielding and 5) receiving. Each level brings me closer and deeper into the presence of the Lord. In His presence is where I get restored to be all I need to be for me, my family, and others along my way.

Prayer is my connection to God and my means of communication. It's a two-way street: God talks; I listen, and when I talk, He listens. Even when I don't have the words (and many times last year, I did not), my prayer language was a communication tool.

Fasting is my detoxification of the flesh and outer influences of toxicity. Fasting allows me to get clean and empty before the Lord so He can fill me up with more of Him. Being able to hear God clearly is key to your restoration.

Singing/Praise is my fuel to keep pressing. Getting lost in song unto the Lord is a pastime I will always enjoy. It strengthens me and allows my heart to love Jesus in a fulfilling way.

Yielding is my posture to receive from God. Once I've been cleansed and detoxed, I hear Him clearly. I lose myself in Him through singing and praising Him. I am ready. I am completely yielded to God for Him to build me back up.

Receiving is my replenishment. I receive all God has for me to continue the journey, but I also receive all He wants me to give to the kingdom, His people, and my family. This part reminds me, my life is not my own. I am sent here to also help others through their troubles.

Yes, I had some hits in 2020. Yes, some of those hits hurt, but I survived. We survived. I found the God of comfort through my worship. He comforted me, fortified me, and restored me to be a comfort to someone else. My testimony is:

> Blessed be the God and Father of our Lord Jesus Christ, the Father of sympathy (pity and mercy) and the God (who is the Source) of every comfort (consolation and encouragement), who comforts (consoles and encourages) us in every trouble (calamity and affliction), so we may also be able to comfort (console and encourage) those who are in any kind of trouble *or* distress with the comfort (consolation and encouragement), which we ourselves are comforted (consoled and encouraged) by God, (2 Corinthians 1:3-4, AMPC)

Reflection Questions

What are your weapons of worship? How do you bring yourself to a place of restoration?

Warfare Prayer

I declare I am stronger. I am wiser. I am more than a conqueror through Christ Jesus. I **crush** every enemy's assignment and **delete** every plan and tactic of the enemy in Jesus' name. I decree God's comfort and mercies have restored me to help someone else in Jesus' name. I declare the Lord is my comfort and my help in the time of need. I **stomp** the enemy under my feet, and **I take back** all that was stolen from me. No weapon formed against me shall prosper. I place upon myself the armor of the Lord and use my weapon of worship to t**ear down**, **block**, and completely **quench** the arrows and spears of the enemy. In Jesus' name. I **bind** all backlash and retaliation. In Jesus' name. Amen.

Day 16
Staying Focused on God's Will—Distraction Is a Trap!
by Tabitha Jones

For no temptation (no trial regarded as enticing to sin), [no matter how it comes or where it leads] has overtaken you and laid hold on you that is not common to man [that is, no temptation or trial has come to you that is beyond human resistance and that is not adjusted and adapted and belonging to human experience, and such as man can bear]. But God is faithful [to His Word and to His compassionate nature], and He [can be trusted] not to let you be tempted and tried and assayed beyond your ability and strength of resistance and power to endure, but with the temptation He will [always] also provide the way out (the means of escape to a landing place), that you may be capable and strong and powerful to bear up under it patiently. (1 Corinthians 10:13, AMPC)

Let's talk about 2017. I felt as if I was getting hit from every side of my marriage, home, emotions, job, and church! It was so heavy I found myself in prayer frequently while having sobbing sessions. I finally said, "God, in all those situations, I realize the common denominator is me! What am I doing wrong?" I felt as if I was a good wife, mother, sister, and friend. I even helped my husband run the ministry. At the same time, I dealt with unnecessary warfare in my life that I should not have had to deal with. While in prayer one day, Holy Spirit said, "Oh! I finally got your attention!" It wasn't that I didn't have an active prayer life. I even fasted every now and then. I heard Holy Spirit say, "Did I direct or ask you to do all those things that you felt were good ideas? You didn't seek Me, and now your life is a hot mess."

"Seek Me first." You may have heard this in church since you were a child but are you applying it to your life? Lean not to your own understanding. God told me, "Your mind is not healed, delivered, or stable." Trying to be lord over your own life is an ingredient for failure. We have miracle-working power through God, but we often forget about it.

Holy Spirit is such a gentleman, though. He asked me, "Are you now ready for Me to lead your life for real?" I said, "Yes, lead and guide me in every area of my life."

Holy Spirit started teaching me I needed to be healed and delivered as part of my journey. It took the time and patience to allow Him to take over. I learned to say no to many things and situations and had to get use to change. Change can be challenging, especially when dealing with old mindsets or stubborn generational curses. But as I began to let Holy Spirit take the lead and drive my life, the stress, headaches, weight, and pressure were slowly being alleviated. It was a process. I had to change to get God's results. I had to be God-positioned to receive God's blessings and see His mighty hand at work. Many individuals didn't like the changes I was making, but what was more important was God's will being done in my life. I realized my marriage, family, and ministry were out of control because those circumstances had me distracted. Distraction is a weapon the enemy tries to use on us regularly. We can't allow breaches or doors to be open that will let Him in.

Ultimately, God must lead every part of our lives. He is a lamp unto my feet and a light unto my path (Psalm 119:105). After I surrendered and stopped trying to help God, He cleared the clutter slowly. I am still in the process, but God getting the glory means more to me than anything.

Reflection Question

What specific actions are you going to take to reduce and eliminate distractions in your life?

Warfare Prayer

Father, in the name of Jesus, show me Your perfect will for my life. Give me clear insight, clarity, and discernment for my life. **Crush** and **annihilate** any traps, people in my ears, heart, and spirit to get me off course. I pray scriptures and prayers lead my emotions and clarity of thought. **Set ablaze** any words I utter that don't align Your plans, decisions, destiny, and will for my life. **Sever** any hindrances I do not see. Make my heart pure in every decision I make. Create in me a clean heart and renew a right spirit in me. I decree and declare my mind, body, and spirit always desire to be submissive and obedient to the Holy Spirit and Jehovah's leading. I **bind** all backlash and retaliation. In Jesus' mighty name. Amen.

Day 17
Mind Checks
by Bejahda Lovelace

"Keep and guard your heart with all vigilance and above all that you guard, for out of it flow the springs of life" (Proverbs 4:23, AMPC).

Have you ever noticed how much you are flooded with waves of various thoughts? Doing frequent mind checks is crucial as we maneuver throughout the day. So many times, and all too often, our minds are bombarded by all types of thoughts. Thoughts of faithlessness, worry, or fear, may cause us to be sad, frustrated, or annoyed. Questions like, "Do I have enough money to pay my bills? Are my children safe in the schools? Am I good enough or smart enough?" may cause us to worry or doubt. You may wonder if your husband/wife loves you. You may be afraid you cannot provide for your family, or your job may become phased out. When these thoughts come, it's mind check time.

One key God has impressed on me is recognizing this is an attack on my mind. Secondly, I must identify what type of attack it is. The more accurately we can identify the spirit behind an attack, the better our ability to eradicate it precisely. Lastly, all enemy attacks should be pulled down quickly. I noticed my mind attacks didn't come big and bad. Trumpets didn't blow when an attack came. Instead, they came very subtly. Anger, for example, would start with a mild annoyance. Then, if I didn't pull that down, it grew to aggravation. If I still did nothing about it, it grew to anger, and if nothing was done, it turned into full-on rage. But God gives believers weapons and a promise. In 2 Corinthians 10:4-8 the Bible says, "For the weapons of our warfare are not physical [weapons of flesh and blood], but they are mighty before God for the overthrow and destruction of strongholds" (KJV), God has also given us armor. Ephesians 6:11-18 states:

> Stand therefore [hold your ground], having tightened the belt of truth around your loins and having put on the breastplate of integrity and of moral rectitude and right standing with God, and having shod your feet in preparation [to face the enemy with the firm-footed stability, the promptness, and the readiness produced by the good news] of the Gospel of peace. [Isaiah 52:7.] Lift up over all the [covering] shield of saving faith, upon which you can quench all the flaming missiles of the wicked [one]. And take the helmet of salvation and the sword that the Spirit wields, which is the Word of God. Pray at all times (on every occasion, in every season) in the Spirit, with all [manner of] prayer and entreaty. To that end, keep alert and watch with strong purpose and perseverance, interceding on behalf of all the saints (God's consecrated people). (AMPC)

Our heavenly Father has said these weapons will protect us and give us victory against every attack of the enemy. I have also been taught by my mentor and spiritual mother, Yvette Benton how to declare. Making declarations has been a lethal weapon against the enemy's attacks.

Remember, the faster we can identify the type of attack, the quicker we can eradicate it. Thus, we leave ourselves open to the truth of what God's Word has to say about the lies the enemy is always trying to make us believe. I have also realized as I am binding up and shutting down the thoughts or suggestions the enemy attempts to plant in my mind, the more empowered I feel in my natural body and spirit. Romans 12:2 says, "Do not be conformed to this world but be transformed by the renewing of your mind that by testing you may discern the will of God." We win the battle of our minds by testing the things we hear and see against God's Word, praying God's Word and operating with discernment and knowledge of God's good, acceptable, perfect will for our lives.

Reflection Questions

1. What does Jesus Christ say we should think about?
2. What must you do to do a better job in this area?

Warfare Prayer

Father God, with the power and authority You have given me, I **set ablaze** every attack of the enemy against my mind. I **reject, shatter,** and **take authority** over every thought the enemy attempts to infiltrate my mind with. I **annihilate** it in the name of Jesus. Your Word tells us we have the mind of Christ (1 Corinthians 2:14-16); we think as Jesus think. You also tell us we have the power to **cast down** imaginations and every high thing that exalts itself against the knowledge of God and bring into captivity every thought to the obedience of Christ (2 Corinthians 10:5). I release a sound mind, a mind focused on You, God. I choose to think about things above and not on things below. In the name of Jesus. I receive and accept that setting my mind on the flesh is death but to set the mind on the Spirit is life and peace. I decree and declare there will be no backlash or retaliation against this prayer. In the name of Jesus. Amen.

Day 18
Victory over Depression by Exposing the Enemy's Lies
by Kelley McLean

"The Lord is close to those who are of a broken heart and saves such as are crushed with sorrow for sin and are humbly and thoroughly penitent. Many evils confront the [consistently] righteous, but the Lord delivers him out of them all" (Psalm 34:18-19, AMPC).

I was leaving the post office after dropping off packages for my latest business venture. It looked as if things were turning around from the outside, but I was actually smack dab in a rock-bottom moment.

The previous two years included transition and trauma topped off with a hormonal roller coaster. In that short time, we had our first child, got married, moved, and learned we were expecting our second child when our first was just eight months. I was just coming to terms with being a stay-at-home mom, which I'd previously decided was not for me. Toward the end of my second pregnancy, I discovered my husband and best friend I trusted had slept with another woman. At that point, the fragile ground I'd been standing on completely fell from under me.

I remember walking to the mailbox with my 18-month-old one day and asking, "God, why have You forsaken me?" I heard the Holy Spirit reply, "Why have you forsaken Me?" Unfortunately, it was true. Somehow, I'd fallen into the trap that milestones and accomplishments would bring me identity and fulfillment. I was becoming a wife, instead of a girlfriend, becoming a mom, and earning degrees in preparation to take the corporate world by storm. None of these things gave me what I longed for in my life. About a year after having my daughter, I was diagnosed with PMDD, a hormonal disorder that made managing my mood seemingly impossible.

As I mentioned, from the outside, things were looking better. My husband was remorseful and tried to pour into me spiritually. We bought our first home, and I was able to stay home with my children while running a business. But I hadn't addressed the root cause of my turmoil. None of these external and temporal things could heal the spiritual wounds that were manifesting and creating the perfect breeding ground for depression. I tried to work out my feelings of inadequacy, drink to cope with the debilitating sorrow, and create an identity as an entrepreneur so I wouldn't be "just a mom."

My husband would read the Bible to me some nights to get the Word into me like an IV drip, but I had decided his efforts were useless. The lies the enemy had been telling me for months had started to take root, and I no longer recognized them as lies. I was convinced my family would not only be okay without me but they would be better off without me. I thought my kids were too young to be genuinely affected by my absence and my husband could remarry a "Mary Poppins" type to fill the motherly role I seemed to lack.

So, that day, as I headed out of the post office's parking lot, a thought crossed my mind. "If you take your foot off the brake, you could roll into oncoming traffic. I can be all over, and it would look like an accident." The thought was so compelling and inviting, I slowly began to lift my foot off the brake. Suddenly, another thought came in louder: "But what if the person who hits you gets hurt or dies. What if there are children in the car? What if you don't die but are just worse off than you are now." I quickly slammed my foot on the brake and carefully and tearfully drove home.

I didn't get here overnight, and I didn't get healed overnight. I realized I needed help, and I sought treatment for my hormones through medication and therapy. While this was enough to see a slither of light through the clouds, I knew if I wanted to truly be set free and delivered from the web of depression, I would have to take on the enemy and his lies full force. I had to surrender my life to my heavenly Father.

Here are the three main lies the devil will use to keep you depressed. I want to help you expose these lies so you can come against them and defeat them.

Lie #1: *"You are not enough."*

The enemy will try to convince you that you are not equipped or prepared enough to handle whatever you are going through or even things you have been blessed with. Whether it's motherhood, being a wife, your career, or ministry, this lie will magnify it if there is any feeling of inadequacy. Satan uses the trick that you are simply not enough to overcome, succeed, or excel in these areas. The purpose of this trick is to keep you focused on your own inadequacies, instead of God's power in your life.

But God! Ephesians 2:10 says we are God's handiwork, created in Christ Jesus to do good works, which God prepared in advance for us to do (NIV). We know we serve an awesome God who knows and designed us when He created us for the works He intends to do. When we rely on our own power and might and follow our own plans, then we can open ourselves to this lie, but when we are aligned in the roles God has ordained for us to do, there's no way the enemy should be able to tell us we aren't enough. We were prepared by a God who is more than enough!

Lie #2: *"It will always be like this."*

Whether you're dealing with depression, grief, or a really difficult season, the enemy will try to magnify your pain and convince you it will last forever, and there is no way out. The trick with this lie is to convince you the pain you are experiencing will never end. The purpose of this lie is to keep you focused on the pain and away from the pain reliever, your heavenly Father.

The Bible tells us in Psalm 34:18-19, "The Lord is close to the brokenhearted and saves those who are crushed in spirit. The righteous person may have many troubles, but the Lord delivers him from them all." How powerful is it that God is close to us when we are at our worst moments, ready to deliver us! But in these moments when God is close to us, are we close to Him? Just because someone is close to you physically doesn't mean you acknowledge or connect with him. Your spouse or child can be sitting right next to you watching TV, but that doesn't mean you're having a conversation with him. You must be willing to trust that trouble will not always last because, as God's Word says, He will deliver you from many troubles. This shows the thought that "It will always be like this" is a lie. You must combat this lie by acknowledging God's presence and His ability to deliver you from the pain.

Lie #3: *"Things will be better without you."*

I believe this lie is at the root of many suicidal attacks. The enemy tries to convince people to alleviate their pain and their absence would better serve those around them. When I look back at the time the enemy had me convinced by his lies, I'm stunned that I could ever believe my children would be better without me. He wanted to rob them of our bond and everything God intends for me to pour into them. He tried to rob my husband of full restoration in our marriage and having me as a Helpmeet as God ushers him into his purpose. The devil comes to steal, kill, and destroy, and he wants to do all three with this lie.

But the biggest trick of this lie is to get us to take matters into our own hands to separate us from God. He wants to kill the purpose and destiny for which God created us. He wants to end things short of the victory God intends for us. But God knows the plans He has for you, plans to prosper you and not to harm you, plans to give you hope and a future (Jeremiah 29:11).

All of these lies serve one purpose: to distract you from God. Whether we live or die, satan desires to keep us from eternal fellowship with our heavenly Father. I encourage you to have victory over any of these lies you may have been receiving. The Bible tells us in James 4:7 when we (1) submit ourselves to God and (2) resist the enemy, satan must flee from us. Satan has no real power, but he is a manipulator and will keep us in his web of lies as long as we let him by convincing us we must stay there. You don't have to wait there. He had no right to put you there in the first place. Decide today you will no longer allow him to interfere with your thoughts.

Reflection Questions

1. What lies have the enemy been telling you in this season?
2. How can you combat these lies with the Word of God?

Warfare Prayer

I repent for anything I have done or my family has done to open myself up to the spirit of depression. I **close** any doors that give the enemy access to my thoughts and emotions. I identify and **come against** the strategies of the enemy to keep me from complete submission to God. I commit to walking in complete alignment and surrender to God in every area of my life.

Depression, sadness, and suicidal thoughts do not have control over my life. I **rebuke** the enemy's plots and plans to destroy my family and me through my mental and emotional health. I declare I have a sound mind and peace that surpasses all understanding. The Lord, my God, is my Comforter and is near to me even when I am brokenhearted and low in spirit. I **resist** the enemy; therefore, he must flee from me (James 4:7). I **break, destroy,** and **shut down** any mental and emotional strongholds in my bloodline. I declare my family and I are delivered and set free from the generational curse of depression and mental and emotional disorders. I declare I already have the victory in Jesus' name because Jesus has given me authority over all the power of the enemy, and nothing shall in any way harm me (Luke 10:19). I **come against** and **cancel** the enemy's lies about my marriage, children, and me. Not only do I take hold and refute the enemy's lies, but I also declare I will believe the report of the Lord. His report says that I am healed, enough, and more than a conqueror (Romans 8:37). I declare I know my Father's voice and will not follow a stranger's voice (John 10:4-5). I will stand on these declarations until I see total victory over the assignment of depression. I will not judge by how I feel or how things appear (2 Corinthians 5:7). I declare I will not lean unto my own understanding. I will acknowledge God in all my ways, and He shall direct my paths (Proverbs 3:5-6). I am free in Christ! I

cancel any backlash and retaliation. In Jesus' name. Amen!

Day 19
Faithfulness
by Chalonda McQueen

"She vowed, saying, O Lord of hosts, if You will indeed look on the affliction of Your handmaid and [earnestly] remember, and not forget Your handmaid but will give me a son, I will give him to the Lord all his life; no razor shall touch his head" (1 Samuel 1:11, AMPC).

Hannah (whose name means grace or favor) was one of the two wives of Elkanah. Peninnah (which means coral or pearl) was the other. Hannah was barren; Peninnah had children.

Annually, Elkanah and his family would leave their hometown to offer sacrifices and worship. Peninnah vexed Hannah because of her barren condition. Elkanah offered sacrificial portions to both wives but gave Hannah more as she had no children. To that effect, Hannah wept and wouldn't eat.

After the sacrificial meal, Hannah went to the temple to pray. Eli, the priest, was sitting at the temple's entrance. He watched her mouth but heard no sounds. He rebuked her, assuming she was drunk. Hannah explained she was praying from the abundance of her sorrows. She was not drunk. Eli blessed her and sent her in peace.

After some time, Hannah became pregnant with and birthed Samuel. After she weaned him, she took him to the annual offering at the temple. She reminded Eli who she was and showed that God had answered her prayers. She left her son Samuel at the temple with Eli, the priest as she had promised. She made and brought him clothes as he grew. She consistently kept her vow and commitment as a mother.

Because of Hannah's faithfulness, God blessed her with three sons and two daughters.

My oldest daughter had a congenital heart defect called Tetralogy of Fallot or blue baby syndrome. I knew something was wrong when she had an ultrasound at four months old. I was terrified. I shouldn't have known looking at the ultrasound that anything was wrong. I don't have any training or expertise in that area. The medical staff seemed alarmed. I couldn't tell if they were alarmed by the picture or that I knew. I prayed and prayed, fasted and prayed. Her surgery was performed when she was three months old. The doctor who performed it was world-renowned. His level of expertise far exceeded the hospital that served us. He greeted and reassured us on the day of surgery with the scripture, "My heart is fixed O, God" (Psalm 57:7). The surgery was beyond successful, and recovery was speedy. Except for the small scar, there's no obvious indication of the whole ordeal. She'll require some future repairs for maintenance and will live an otherwise long and healthy life.

Reflection Questions

1. How can you build trust in God in impossible circumstances?
2. How can you steward the promises God gives you and remain faithful to keep your promise to Him after He delivers?

Warfare Prayer

I declare I will seek God first concerning impossibilities in my life and expect His blessings. I won't lean on my understanding but trust Him to direct and provide. I will remain faithful to the terms/conditions of my promise, regardless. I decree that God can trust me to correctly steward the blessings He's given me to honor and praise Him for all His kindness to me. I declare my focus is on God, not on my circumstances. I **annihilate** the spirits of fear and destroy trauma. I declare I am victorious. I **crush** the victim spirit. I am an overcomer by the blood and word of my testimony. I **bind** all backlash and retaliation. In Jesus' name. Amen.

Day 20
The Valley Experience
by Melinda Nicholson

"They cried to You and were delivered; they trusted in, leaned on, and confidently relied on You, and were not ashamed or confounded or disappointed" (Psalm 22:5, AMPC).

Have you ever had a situation you prayed about but still found yourself engulfed by it? I have and probably some of you have too. My grandmother called it "between a rock and a hard place," but I like to call it a "valley experience." Whatever you choose to call the situation, it is a place you really do not want to be. Some examples of the valley experience look like depression, suicide ideology, domestic violence, rape, incest, infidelity, divorce, rejection, abandonment, verbal abuse, deception, gluttony, and the list could go on and on.

Sometimes we get ourselves into the valley experience, and sometimes the valley experience finds us. The funny thing about the valley experience is it just does not affect one situation. Still, it affects various areas of our existence. We are products of our environment and experiences, whether good or bad. They shape our views of how we see things and react to situations. Have you ever met someone for the first time and had a negative perception of her for some reason? In my day, we would say she seems stuck up or guarded. Is it possible she has not dealt with the stress and pressures of her valley experience? We often carry the weight of our valley experiences and nurse them until they turn us into people we don't even like. The enemy is crafty that way, and he knows how to make us justify why we have the right to nurse the hurts of the past. The weight will soon become unbearable until it controls our very thought process. Therefore, we must renounce the enemy's lies that will keep us in the bondage of shame, humiliation, and disgrace.

This is how Merriam-Webster defines shame:

1. A painful feeling of humiliation or distress caused by the consciousness of wrong or foolish behavior; Verb (of a person, action, or situation) make (someone) feel ashamed

This is how the Vine's Expository Dictionary defines shame:

1. The Greek word is atimia, and it means dishonor, shame, reproach

Can you imagine having a painful feeling of shame, humiliation, distress, disgrace, and dishonor? Have you experienced gut-wrenching pain that kept you up late night after night? I don't have to imagine it because I have lived it. I have cried out to God many nights out of despair asking him to please take the pain away! "God, please move me out of this valley. God are You hearing me?"

Then, I heard God say to me, "Be still and know that I am God." What I discovered through my valley experience was that God heard me, but He required something of me first. I had to surrender to His will and His way of doing things. I realized prayer and worry cannot reside in the same place. Therefore, my prayers were going amiss. He never meant for me to bear this burden alone. God said in His Word to cast your cares on Him because He cares for you. By surrendering to God, the plank from my eyes was removed for me to receive God's grace that sustained me even as I was going through my valley experience!

I want to encourage you that God's grace will sustain you in your valley experience. Just cry out to God and surrender your burden to Him. God is bigger than any valley experience anyone will ever face. All we must do is keep our faith and focus on God because "with God all things are possible." Only then will we start to feel God's presence and experience His true comfort that comes through the Holy Spirit. Press through. Walk by faith and not by sight until you touch the hem of His garment to be made whole. Then, you will receive God's goodness, kindness, mercy, and grace!

It is God's grace and mercy that will elevate you to a sweet spot to rise above your valley experience. The beauty of God is present, even though you are still in the valley. You now have peace that surpasses all understanding. Instead of being engulfed by the valley experience, you can rest on the promises of God!

I leave you with three things to meditate on when you are in a valley experience:

1. God will never leave you or forsake you (Hebrews 13:5)
2. God's grace is sufficient (2 Corinthians 12:9)
3. God will work all things together for our good (Romans 8:28)

God loves us, and it is in the valley that we grow!

Reflection Questions

1. What valley experience are you dealing with currently?
2. What are you doing about your valley experience?

Warfare Prayer

Father God, I come in the mighty name of Jesus and the power of Your Holy Spirit within me to **take authority** over and **shut down** the spirit of shame and humiliation. Your Word says to cry out, and I will be saved; trust You, and I will not be put to shame (Psalm 22:5). **I send Holy Ghost fire** and **set ablaze** the spirit of disgrace and dishonor that will no longer keep me in bondage. I declare and decree You did not give me a spirit of fear but of power, love, and a sound mind (2 Timothy 1:7). I stand on Your Word that greater is He in me than he that is in the world (1 John 4:4). I take the sword of the Spirit, uproot generational curses, and **dismantle** the enemy's assignments to close all entry portals. I loose boldness in the spirit and stand on the promise of God that I can do all things through Christ who gives me strength (Philippians 4:13). I declare and decree healing is my portion. There will be nothing missing, nothing lacking, no backlash or retaliation. I seal this declaration covered with the whole armor of God and the blood of Jesus. Amen!

Day 21
I Am My Father's Child, and I Look Just Like My Daddy!
by Tabetha Pittman

"So God created man in His own image, in the image *and* likeness of God He created him; male and female He created them" (Genesis 1:27, AMPC).

When elevations are coming, when you give God your yes and start walking toward your kingdom purpose and His perfect will, the adversary always comes harder and meaner. His plan is to make you just give up and stop. The Bible tells us the world will start to bombard our minds with unbelief and tell us the opposite of what the Father has said. The world will do anything to stop us from believing and to keep us from seeing the light of the gospel of the glory of Christ. He will play games with our minds, affect our bodies and outer appearances, so we'll think we're not the image of God (2 Corinthians 4:3-4, ESV).

Satan's job is to tempt us into coming off our post and tell us to look at the scars that are making us ugly. The enemy will have us thinking, "Who would want someone like you?" You'll start looking at yourself in the mirror negatively. He attacks your self-esteem, makes you not want to be around anyone, to be a hermit, timid and unworthy of the things of God. The spirit of depression, comparison, competition, anger, and rebellion is dancing all around you. You're in a sunken place. He got you, boo. Satan is winning. He has done his job.

I'm not sure how God deals with you, but He talks to me straight, no chaser.

My child, stop tripping and being dramatic. What did I say you are? Are you looking at yourself as I see you, or are you using your fleshly eyes? I made you beautiful, and My vision of you is not of the world. I said you were healed, and everything you've lost, I'll replace. Do you believe Me? I said you would get your swagger back. Believe in My time. Isn't My grace sufficient enough? Stop asking Me questions you already know the answer to. Stop asking Me the same questions repeatedly. You know the answer. I said I am rebuilding, replacing, and strengthening you. That's what I meant.

When in doubt about what God has already promised and spoken over you, stop and think. All God asks of you is to continue to do His will. Continue to walk in His light and purpose. Even while you're waiting for His promises to manifest, carry yourself as if it's already done. People will ask, "How do you do it? How did you get through it with such grace and dignity?" With the smile you carry on your face, people will not even know what you're dealing with in your life. But you will do it because you know God loves you. His love will carry you through anything. Do not be ashamed of His masterpiece. You are His handy work. Everything He makes with His hands is a work of art.

Reflection Question

Look in the mirror. Describe at least five beautiful features about yourself that you see.

Out of your mouth declare: "I have been fearfully and wonderfully made in the image of my Father" (Psalm 139:14, AMPC).

Warfare Prayer

My Father, I humbly yet boldly come to Your throne of grace sitting at Your feet. I use the full authority You have granted me to **decapitate** and **sever** all negative images the enemy speaks to me. I'm **pulling all negative thoughts, words, and memories up from the root** and casting Holy Ghost fire against the lies the world says that my body must look beautiful. I receive the power and understanding that what I see is the wonderful person my Father made. Never will I question why I look the way I do or how valuable I am to God's perfect plan. When I look at the birds of the air, they neither sow, reap nor gather into barns, and yet my heavenly Father feeds them. Am I not of more value than them (Matthew 6:26)? I control my feelings and emotions as my Father said I shall not become discouraged (utterly spiritless, exhausted, and weary because of fear). What I have come to understand is though our outer man is [progressively] decaying *and* wasting away, yet, our inner self is being [progressively] renewed day after day (2 Corinthians 4:16). I understand with my whole heart I am blessed and that my Lord will fulfill His promises to me (Luke 1:45). I received God's grace before the foundation of the world, As it is written, God saw everything that He created, including us. Then, He was able to rest because it was all very good (Genesis 1:31). I am my Father's good thing, and I bind all backlash and retaliation. In Jesus' name. Amen.

Day 22
It's Not About You
by Nikki Purcell

"And He said to all, if any person wills to come after Me, let him deny himself [disown himself, forget, lose sight of himself and his own interests, refuse and give up himself] and take up his cross daily and follow Me [cleave steadfastly to Me, conform wholly to My example in living and, if need be, in dying also]" (Luke 9:23, AMPC).

Travel with me as we take this journey that all started in my childhood and manifested in my marriage. At the age of 18, I decided I would be alone because relationships hurt too deeply. I knew what hurt felt like, and I never wanted to experience that type of pain again. The song that comes to mind is "When Somebody Loves You Back." That's all I wanted. I knew God loved me, but having that physical touch and acceptance was what I lacked. I decided to just enjoy life and never settle again. My mind was made up, but God had another plan.

One summer in college, I met my husband. He caught my eye, and I caught his. But in my head, I wasn't looking, and I wasn't going to play games. Something was different about this man though. He was everything I once prayed for, but again, I wasn't going to settle. We started dating and had a great time together. He was like a dream come true to me, but it all seemed unreal. He poured his heart out to me. He took me out and treated me like a queen. He opened doors for me. We went to church every Sunday and enjoyed doing life together. I was truly living my best life. It felt good to have someone pour into me for once without sucking the life out of me. He gave me his time and his heart. I was happy.

We eventually got married, and I felt entitled. I thought it had to be my way or no way. I realized I wasn't compromising. Well, I did in my head, but I had an attitude about it later. I wasn't adaptable, encouraging, or supportive, but I was a nagger. This wasn't God, and it wasn't okay. This pattern of control and selfishness cost me happiness in my marriage for years. I viewed my spouse as not providing what I needed. However, I had to start looking at why I was so demanding and had to have things my way. As I look back, I understand this spirit came way before my husband. This wasn't my husband's fault. He had been doing all he knew to do as my husband, but even that wasn't good enough for me at the time. Looking to anyone besides God to complete me was so far from His will.

I cried out for help, and God heard me. The Helpmeet Army literally changed my life forever. Plus, it saved my marriage because it saved me. I can stand today and say I have successfully rebuilt my relationship with my husband, and selfishness is no longer a part of our lives. We serve one another without question. His needs come before mine, and my needs come before his. This can only be done when God is in a relationship because this isn't natural at all. Naturally, we want our desires met; however, we must deny ourselves first.

Reflection Questions

1. What is God asking and requiring of you?
2. Did something happen in your childhood that caused you to be selfish? Explain. Get rid of it so you can be free today.

Warfare Prayer

Father, in the name of Jesus, I **burn up** selfishness. I **force it out** with the Word of God. Selfishness is not my portion. I **command** selfishness to have no place in my heart. The Word of God states we should love one another as Christ has loved us (John 15:12). The Lord is our Shepherd; we shall not want (Psalm 23:1). Create in me a clean heart, O God, and renew a right spirit within me (Psalm 51:10). No longer will we think everything is about us and our needs. We must see the bigger picture. God needs us to get free so we can help others. Selfishness isn't part of the fruit of the Spirit, so it must go. God is our provider, and we must share our hearts, service, time, money, and resources with those God has placed in our lives. We release selfishness, and replace it with generosity. Generosity is our portion, and we walk in it. You will be enriched in every way to be generous in every way, which through us will produce thanksgiving to God (2 Corinthians 9:11). I **cancel** backlash and retaliation. In the name of Jesus. Amen.

Day 23
Stand Ground
by Alkesha Rogers

"For we are not wrestling with flesh and blood [contending only with physical opponents], but against the despotisms, against the powers, against [the master spirits who are] the world rulers of this present darkness, against the spirit forces of wickedness in the heavenly (supernatural) sphere" (Ephesians 6:12, AMPC).

During my stand for marital restoration, I had to learn that the separation time was not just so my husband could get his "act together" but so God could get *my* "act together." As I grew stronger in my relationship with God, I realized my marital problems were just a "distraction" the enemy used to try to keep me from fulfilling my God-given purpose. I always responded to a negative comment or an act of disrespect or dishonesty from my husband with anger and rage. I would focus on my husband as my opponent. It wasn't until I learned the meaning of the scripture, "For we fight not against flesh and blood but against spiritual forces of wickedness" (Ephesians 6:12), that I realized this battle I was chosen to fight was not against my husband. The enemy was my main opponent. More importantly, the battle was already won! Once I realized this, I was armed and dangerous. The enemy didn't have a chance. I fought differently.

God has given us the ability and power to change our mindsets and to recognize the enemies' schemes, plots, tricks, and plans that he uses to throw us off focus. We must put on the complete armor of

God daily to stand firm and fight against any and all distractions.

Reflection Question

What strategies do you use when the enemy throws distractions your way to throw you off track from the promises of God?

Warfare Prayer

Father, in the name of Jesus, I use my power and authority to recognize every plot, trick, and plan the enemy tries to use to distract me from my God-given purpose. I **destroy** every assignment of distraction and will stand firm and fight. Your Word declares we must "Put on the full armor of God so that we shall be able to resist and stand ground" (Ephesians 6:13). I decree and declare my destiny and goals will rise above all forms of distractions. I **cut down** the enemy's plan to hold me captive to my assignment, and I will achieve what You have called me to do. I can do all things through Christ, which strengthens me (Philippians 4:13). Lord, I will not stop pursuing what You have told me to do until all has been achieved for Your glory. I **bind** all backlash and retaliation. In Jesus' name. Amen.

Day 24
The Silent Rejection
by Rose Rome Hammond

"For the weapons of our warfare are not physical [weapons of flesh and blood], but they are mighty before God for the overthrow and destruction of strongholds" (2 Corinthians 10:4, AMPC).

As a young teenager, I looked more mature than I actually was. My mom would allow me to babysit for a young lady who was about 10 years my senior. I would keep her three boys when she went out to party. This exposed me to adult circumstances I wasn't actually maturely ready to experience. Plus, our relationship grew from the babysitter to me being in one of the gangs, unbeknownst to my mother. This young lady was a very popular person, and her place was where her friends gathered. Her friends assumed I was of legal age, which at that time was eighteen years old, although I was five years short of being old enough. I met a young man at the neighbor's house who was a nice guy; he would show me some attention. The relationship progressed to a sexual relationship, but the interest he had for me dissipated. From that one-time encounter with the young man, I was pregnant.

As a young girl, I was unprepared to handle this situation and too afraid and embarrassed to tell my parents, so I turned to my neighbor. My neighbor was with me when I told the young man about the pregnancy. There was silence, and then he questioned how I could be pregnant. We were only together once. It was at that time I learned he was in a committed relationship with another woman. I realized at that moment I was in this predicament alone. So, I broke the news to my parents, and they were very disappointed. However, my adopted father broke the awkward moment and voiced support for me through the circumstances. Being pregnant at such a young age was less than ideal. I dealt with a lot of mental torment and embarrassment surrounding the circumstances of my pregnancy. Many days, I wished I was older, in a loving, supportive, and stable married relationship, where the timing would be perfect for bringing a child into the world. Now, as I think back on the circumstances surrounding my own conception, they were not very different from the one I was facing. My mother was separated from her first husband when I was conceived. My biological father was not interested in a committed relationship and having a baby at that time. Therefore, my mother had to deal with the circumstances on her own. I believe my mom wished she had different circumstances during her pregnancy with me. She wanted things to be different. It has been said babies can feel the emotional stress of being unwanted or, in my case, wanting different circumstances for the pregnancy. In that silent rejection, the enemy is a legalist. He took that moment where I wished for different circumstances during my pregnancy to plant the seed of rejection in me. I was now passing it to the next generation.

My life experiences were shaped by the spirit of rejection from birth to adulthood. Many of the rejection attributes were so entwined in my personality I accepted them as my own and did very little to change them. The call of God for me to take a stand for my marriage was new territory for me. When dealing with anything that looked like rejection, my usual response was to take the defensive route and cut my losses. But this time, God pulled the love card for Him that stopped me in my tracks. Which was 1

John 5:3: "For the [true] love of God is this: that we do His commands [keep His ordinances and are mindful of His precepts and teaching]." And these orders of His are not irksome (burdensome, oppressive, or grievous). This was my earliest revelation of God's Word with understanding. I knew when I was walking in Love with God and when I wasn't. It was a point in my life that I desired to love God. So, I prayed and asked God to put a mentor in my life for every area I was to fill his perfect will. Shortly after my prayer, a friend tagged me on a Facebook live of Yvette Benton. She was giving a testimony about how God transformed her to be the testimony that turned her husband's heart back to Him. Now, they are both fulfilling the purpose of God for their lives.

I knew she had what I needed to obey God's will for my own relationship. I started meeting with her for counseling and later felt led to join the Helpmeet Army's mentoring group under the Holy Spirit's leadership and teaching. This mentorship program is for those who are serious about learning who God is and who they are in Him. I am discovering His perfect will for me and how He equipped us for the battle against the principalities of darkness that fight to keep us from fulfilling His perfect will. I became more aware of the hindering spirits like rejection and learned how to use spiritual weapons in spiritual war. I have chopped off the head of rejection, but God teaches me how to go after the root of life and be the bloodline breaker for my entire family.

Reflection Question

What is keeping you from fulfilling God's perfect will in your life? What do you need to do to address this issue?

Warfare Prayer

God, I thank You for Your revelation of the knowledge of who You are and who I am in You. I forgive my ancestors for passing that spirit down to me and **renounce** rejection from my life. I **demolish** the magnification of rejection and its sense of being unwanted and unable to receive love from others. I **break free** from perfectionism, fear, withdrawing from life, pride, self-reliance, people-pleasing, lust, insecurity, inferiority, shame, and anger with the authority of God's consuming Holy Ghost fire. There is, therefore, now no condemnation for me in Christ Jesus. "For the law of the Spirit of life has set me free in Christ Jesus from the law of sin and death" (Romans 8:2). "I declare the freedom of Christ has set me free; stand firm therefore, and do not submit again to a yoke of slavery" (Galatians 5:1). With Christ and the authority He has given me, I **break** the enemy's hold, and he must flee and catch fire. In the name of Jesus. Your Word says, "The Spirit of the Lord GOD is upon me because the LORD has anointed me" (Isaiah 61:1, ESV). Because my God holds me in His love, I am free, free, and free! I **bind** all backlash and retaliation! In Jesus' name. Amen.

Day 25
I Surrender All
by Carla Shelton

"I appeal to you therefore, brethren, and beg of you in view of [all] the mercies of God, to make a decisive dedication of your bodies [presenting all your members and faculties] as a living sacrifice, holy (devoted, consecrated) and well-pleasing to God, which is your reasonable (rational, intelligent) service and spiritual worship" (Romans 12:1, AMPC).

Have you ever stopped to think about what it truly means to surrender all to God? I was clueless about the requirements until I was faced with one of the most challenging times of my life.

It was a Monday afternoon, and I was at my wit's end. I'd cried, yelled, and explained my case to everyone who would listen. I was completely drained. In a matter of weeks, everything I knew to be my peace and happiness was disrupted, transformed, and ultimately destroyed in my mind. I could not understand it, and I was going crazy trying to understand why. How could my seemingly perfect life be broken so quickly? I needed to get it back on track so my life could get back to being normal. No matter what I tried, nothing was working. I was losing control, and I didn't like it. What was going on? At that moment, I heard a voice in my spirit which said, "Now, do I have your attention?" I heard it and ignored it.

I didn't think twice about the small still voice until months later.

Time started to pass, but things didn't get better. I continued to stress and worry until I heard the voice again one day; this time, it said, "Seek me!" What was this voice talking about, and why was it talking to me about seeking him? I wasn't sure why I kept hearing the voice. One day, in my despair, I screamed, "What do you mean? Haven't I been seeking you?" The voice said, "How much? You seek me when you need me; you say prayers amidst your issues, but you don't seek me?" At that point, I was upset! The voice actually responded with lies. All types of crazy thoughts started to go through my head. I'm a good person. I'm faithful, accommodating, and dependable. What was I missing? The next several weeks would reveal to me what the still voice was conveying. The Holy Spirit spoke to my heart and gave me the simple instructions to cast my cares on Him. At that moment, repentance fell all over me. I ran into my newly empty closet and began to scream out, "I'm sorry. I'm so sorry. Lord, I hear You. I'll seek You and give my life to You. I'll surrender everything to You."

Over the next couple of months, God came to me, and before I knew it, I was surrendered entirely. The Word became my strength and refuge. The revelation of things I'd ignored as a wife, mother, and friend slowly began to shift, and my heart started to change. As I focused on God and His Word, my life and thoughts began to yield to Him. I gained indescribable trust and peace beyond words. I felt a transformation in my mind, body, and spirit, and I wasn't the same. My old way of thinking was gone, and I wanted to live a life pleasing to God. I couldn't fix it. Surrendering to God gave me the assurance I needed to know He was in control.

Surrendering to God takes strength and courage. It's a personal decision to give up your will while understanding God ultimately controls the outcome.

Reflection Exercise

Describe what you need to do to change your ideas about a fully surrendered lifestyle.

Warfare Prayer

Father God, I come to You in the matchless name of Jesus, declaring I surrender all. I affirm my life is not my own, and it belongs to You. I will not ponder or waver over the call on my life, so I release my will to You. You have full authority over my mind, body, and spirit, and I humbly submit my all to You withholding nothing.

Enemy, I serve notice: you have been **evicted** from my life. I am a child of the highest God who has given me the authority to trample on serpents, so I **stomp**, **crush**, and **annihilate** you before you even come near me. I send you back to the pit of hell where You come from. I will not be moved because I was chosen before I was created in my mother's womb. I am God's masterpiece. Satan, you will no longer torment me with your antiquated games. My God says who the Son sets free is free indeed, so I declare you powerless against me. The Lord promised the enemy who revolts against me will be defeated before me. He will come from one direction and flee in seven. Satan, I resist you, and you must flee. I **cast down** every lie ever spoken over my life, and I **set ablaze** any thoughts that would convince me otherwise. Every wicked scheme or plan you have planned for my life has been dismantled, and I declare you a loser. The Word says I am more than a conquer, and so I walk in victory. I declare neither death nor life, neither angels nor demons, neither the present nor the future, nor any powers, neither height nor depth, nor anything else in all creation, will be able to separate me from the love of God that is in Christ Jesus our Lord. I release a new level of obedience over my life, and I decree and declare all hindrances, distractions, backlash, or retaliation are **destroyed.** In Jesus' name. Amen.

Day 26
Get Up
by Nequia Speaks

"For if you forgive people their trespasses {their reckless and willful sins, leaving them, letting them go, and giving up resentment}, your heavenly Father will also forgive you" (Matthew 6:14, AMPC).

In January of 2018, I was invited to attend the Women's Fellowship at my former church. The woman of God stated, "I heard your name in prayer, and the Lord wanted me to tell you that some questions you've been asking Him in prayer will be answered at the event."

My husband and I weren't together at the time; yet, the Lord gave me specific instructions for restoring my marriage. I was in uncharted territory, so I was definitely in need of answers. The Women's Fellowship was powerful. It was as if everyone came expecting to receive something from the Lord, and God met us there! Midway through the fellowship, Kevin Levar's "A Heart that Forgives" was playing. The minister instructed us to close our eyes and allow the song to speak to us. The woman my husband had been dating was a few tables over. While listening to the song, tears began to flow down my eyes. Holy Spirit began speaking to me, and I was instructed to go over to the young lady and release her from the unforgiveness I held toward her. As I went back and forth with God, asking if I could forgive her from my seat, He said, "Get up." I took a deep breath, said a flash prayer for strength and guidance and walked over to the woman. While the minister was speaking, I motioned for her to stand up. She did, and I reached over and gave her the sincerest hug I could muster. While embracing her, I told her I had released her. At that moment, she held on to me even tighter.

After the embrace, she looked me in my eyes and said, "You take care of them." As I turned to walk away, I stopped mid-stride and said, "What did you say?" She repeated, "You take care of them!" I began crying hysterically and ran to the ladies' room to gather my composure. The other woman followed me into the bathroom, and to my surprise, we had "church" there. After the rejoicing and crying, I asked her what had happened. She said she and my husband had been having difficulties in the relationship since I told him the Lord wanted us to reconcile a few months back. She had come to the Women's Fellowship asking God for clarity on whether or not she should proceed with the relationship. She said she received "confirmation" at the moment I released her from my unforgiveness.

Forgiveness is a decision. At that moment, at that table, I decided to let "it" go. I made a choice to let "her" go. I heard someone say holding on to unforgiveness is like drinking poison, expecting the other person to die! Foolish, right?! I used to live in that place until one day, I found myself in the emergency room with my heart practically beating out of my chest. It was in that hospital room I heard the Lord ask me, "How long are you going to hold on to this?" That's when I decided never to allow unforgiveness to rule my life. Your body will keep the score, and it is not worth it. Choose forgiveness; make it a daily practice. Offenses will come but choose to forgive daily. By maintaining this daily practice, you will remain on the path of freedom.

Reflection Question

What offenses are you choosing to hold on to? Your body will keep the score unforgiveness holds. Release those offenses today. Your breakthrough is at the beginning of forgiveness.

Warfare Prayer

Father God, I **crush** the demonic assignment of unforgiveness! I throw Holy Ghost bombs into the enemy's camp. I **set it ablaze** and **stomp** on its ashes. Your Word declares we are to forgive our brother seventy times seven (Matthew 18:21-22). I **sever** all manner of unforgiveness with the sword of the Spirit. "For God has not given us a spirit of fear, but of power, and of love, and of a sound mind" (2 Timothy 1:7). "Whom the Son has set free is free indeed" (John 8:36). No longer will we be held captive by the hardness of heart. I declare and decree we have the supernatural ability to forgive. Today, we lay aside every weight and sin, which so easily ensnares us, and we choose to let it go. We let it go for ourselves. We let it go for our children, and we let it go for our children's children. Behold, God has done a new thing, and it springs forth now! In Jesus' name.

Day 27
Count the Cost
by Wykehlia Stanley

"Judge not [neither pronouncing judgment nor subjecting to censure], and you will not be judged; do not condemn and pronounce guilty, and you will not be condemned and pronounced guilty; acquit and forgive and release (give up resentment, let it drop), and you will be acquitted and forgiven and released" (Luke 6:37, AMPC).

On the evening of January 8, 2021, I stood in the kitchen, meditating on the unutterable events that had taken place over the past week while making tea. I slowly took a deep breath and stared in horror. I said, "God, no, this can't be!" When I inhaled, I felt shards of glass enter my heart. For a moment, I was paralyzed by what I felt, and then the sting of anger began to manifest. The more I meditated on being let down, the angrier I became.

Sunday morning, I cried out to God and said, "I can't let the enemy stop me from worshipping." Worship was amazing, and I felt a little lighter. I made up my mind I was going to pretend nothing was going on. Service started via Zoom, and I tried everything to get into it. However, the smile I plastered on my face melted like ice cream on hot concrete. What I felt on the inside began to manifest on the outside. The hurt, pain, anger, and shame bubbled up like lava from a volcano waiting to erupt. Before service was over, words of correction came from the Holy Spirit, but something was hindering me from receiving them. That afternoon, I had to interact with my husband, and I was withdrawn and dry in speech. This behavior offended and blindsided him.

When he left, I lost it. I screamed and cried. I wept in agony. "It's not fair," I chanted as I ran and yelled, desperate for the pain to stop. I heard the Holy Spirit say, "Who are you to discount or discard what I have paid for?" Exhausted, I sat in the middle of the floor hoarse and broken-hearted but still holding on to anger. Evening came, and as I sat on the couch, I began to have chest pains as my arm ached. I curled up in the fetal position because I was so angry! Gasping for air, I thought to myself, I can't die because I will go straight to hell. Tears burned my face as they rolled down and hit my chest. At that moment, I asked my Father for forgiveness, and I chose to forgive my husband and myself. The chest pains stopped, and the anger dissipated. I rejoiced because I knew my life had been spared at that moment and my Father loved me too much to allow me to self-destruct.

I was on a fast at the time and asked God about His chosen fast. I was directed to change my fast, and it was during this time, the Holy Spirit revealed I had a residue of unforgiveness attached to new hurts. I put expectations on my husband, instead of relying on my Father. So when my husband did not deliver, I got hurt. I had a choice, but I would not receive God's best for me if I chose anger. I decided to open my mouth and receive my deliverance. I received deliverance because I first had a willing heart that did not want to stay unforgiving. The longer we stay in this state, the more comfortable and bound we become. Next, I asked my Father to forgive and help me because I knew I could not help myself. I was willing to surrender unforgiveness so I could receive my Father's best for me. In return, I was given a pliable heart that loves freely. A warmth engulfed my heart, and a love so pure and tangible overwhelmed me. Deliverance happens differently every time. Sometimes it is instant; other times, it is in stages. We must be aware and constantly pull-down strongholds that come to hinder and distract us from our destinies. We must also do routine self-assessments and be honest about the results. It is a blessing to be delivered from the things that keep us bound, but it is imperative to maintain our freedom. Not maintaining deliverance exposes us to the enemy and strongholds worse than what were previously evicted. Our lives and the lives of those connected to us depend on us.

Reflection Questions

1. Are there any areas of my life with residue?
2. Based on what you have learned from reading today's devotional, what do you need to address any residue you may have?

Warfare Prayer

Father God, in the name of Jesus, I **eradicate** the residue of unforgiveness. I send Holy Ghost fire to saturate and fortify my heart from all hurts. Your Word says, "Be kind and compassionate to one another, forgiving each other, just as in Christ God forgave you" (Ephesians 4:32). I decree and declare I forgive as Christ always forgave me, and I walk in love and kindness. I don't treat others how they treat me, but I display the love of Christ through my words, seeds, and deeds. I **dismantle** the spirits of bitterness, rage, anger, clamor, and evil speaking with all malice (Ephesians 4:31). I have an overflow of pleasantness and delight in my posture, speech, and actions. With the authority You have given me, I **keep guard** of my heart, for out of it flows the springs of life (Proverbs 4:23). I decree and declare regardless of what things look like, sound like or feel like, I maintain a posture of forgiveness. I seal every breach, gap, or unknown entryway with the blood of Jesus. I bind all backlash and retaliation. In Jesus' name. Amen.

Day 28
Faith Moves Mountains
by Darlene Staring

"He said to them, Because of the littleness of your faith [that is, your lack of firmly relying on trust]. For truly I say to you, if you have faith [that is living] like a grain of mustard seed, you can say to this mountain, move from here to yonder place, and it will move; and nothing will be impossible to you" (Matthew 17:20, AMPC).

It was not until my marriage and family fell apart that God began to show me what faith is. God usually shows you these kinds of things when you are in the valley and feel like giving up. I had been through so many forms of rejection in my life, so I told myself this was the last one. If my husband does not want to be with me, then I do not want to live.

The devil is a liar!

Satan almost had me. He tried so hard to destroy me, but God is faithful. When I prayed and cried out to God, I felt Him tell me, "Have faith that I can and will put your marriage back together again." This verse continued to come to my mind repeatedly. Being the research person I am, I began to look up the word "faith." According to The Oxford Dictionary, faith is defined as "complete trust or confidence in someone or something". I thought to myself, "Okay, God, I have faith in you and that you can put my marriage together again." Then I started looking into the

Bible. Do you know there are 79 verses in the Bible relating to faith? As I read them, I began to understand faith is crucial to God.

I then started researching a mustard seed. A mustard seed is only .039 to .079 inches in diameter. That is a very tiny seed. If you only need faith as big as a mustard seed to move a mountain, God is telling us our faith can be exceedingly small to make a difference. I continued with my research. A mustard seed might be very tiny, but when planted, it grows to be 5 to 6.5 feet tall, towering over many other plants—even a tree. The roots go as deep as 5 feet deep. As my research continued, I learned mustard seed plants keep away other pests and weeds that struggle to grow around them. But for the seed to grow, it needs action. The mustard seed must be planted in good soil, and it must be watered, fed, and taken care of properly.

I began to understand why God emphasized a mustard seed and how it related to faith and marriage. I had faith God would not just restore my marriage, but I knew God would make our marriage better than it has ever been. Then God showed me it was not enough to have faith in God to heal and restore my marriage. Sometimes you must take a step out in faith. Even if you are the only one who believes God will do what He said He would do. This requires action. What action? Ask God; He will tell you. You must be obedient to whatever God tells you to do. The Bible says faith without works is dead. God showed me this was not just about my marriage. This was about rescuing my husband from the clutches of the enemy. It was about breaking generational curses that would affect my children, grandchildren, and future generations. This was about changing the lives of many helpmeets.

God told me I needed to plant my faith in good soil. I needed to find a ministry to become a part of that would fight this battle with me. I needed to water and feed my faith. I had to feed on God's Word daily. I needed to speak life into my marriage. I had to stop looking at the natural and the circumstances around me. All these things were distractions the enemy was throwing at me in an attempt to get me to doubt and give up. The one thing satan did not realize is that giving up was never an option for me. I fought this battle for several years for my husband and family. I knew what God had told me. I stood firm in my faith and held on to God's Word and His promises. The more distractions satan threw my way, the more I would dig in my heels and ask God to increase my faith. I would pick up my shield of faith, as well as decree and declare God's Word. I declared this mountain would move and fall into the sea. After 13 years, my mountain did fall into the sea, and my marriage was restored. Hallelujah!

Reflection Questions

1. What mountain are you asking God to move?
2. What actions do you need to take to keep holding onto your faith and believing God can and will do what seems impossible?

Warfare Prayer

Father God, I use the authority You have given me to **come up against** and **crush** doubt and unbelief. Your Word says with You, all things are possible (Matthew 19:26). So, I put on the helmet of salvation and declare our minds are renewed. I **dismantle** any lies of doubt or unbelief the enemy has told me about my situation and that it is impossible. God, Your Word says if we have faith as small as a mustard seed, we can speak to a mountain, and it will move (Matthew 17:20). I **release** my confidence and trust in You, Lord, and declare no good withheld from me. Father, increase my faith. So, I take the shield of faith and declare the mountain we are facing will dissolve into the sea. I bind all backlash and retaliation. In Jesus' name. Amen.

Day 29
Keep the Mind of Christ
by Vonda Warren

"Therefore if any person is [ingrafted] in Christ (the Messiah), he is a new creation (a new creature altogether); the old [previous moral and spiritual condition] has passed away. Behold, the fresh and new has come!" (2 Corinthians 5:17, AMPC).

The Helpmeet role is a lifestyle that requires you to be a watchman. In spiritual warfare, the enemy first wages war in the mind. The mind is a vulnerable place in which many thoughts are generated daily. Many of our fears and insecurities are birthed through our thoughts. I believe, for this reason, Paul encourages us in Romans 12:2 to renew our minds daily. He cautions us not to become so well-adjusted to our culture that we fit into it without even thinking. Fixing our attention on God will change us from the inside out.

The peak of our accomplishments is tied to our level of consistency and commitment to renewing our minds. We must declutter our minds by being conscious of thoughts that waste our time and energy, as these thoughts trigger emotions that can affect our hearts' postures. Thoughts of old ways, past hurts, and the negative advice of others tend to trigger emotions.

For years, I battled thoughts that my words did not matter and someone else had already said it, so why did I need to bother saying it. I felt as if I was stating the obvious. These are lies from the enemy. My thoughts had me more concerned about people's reactions than my obedience to God. I allowed negative thoughts to control what God was nudging me to say and do, which was to assist others by providing solutions. You see, I didn't value the power of my words, but God kept reminding me of my voice and the gifts He placed inside of me. I began writing, recording, and speaking about what God thinks of me. This gave me the courage to speak to others. I soon realized I may not be called to everyone, but someone was listening for my voice.

In conclusion, remember the mind is the container of our thoughts and emotions. It determines the quality of our words and feelings, which are unreliable. Therefore, we must set our affections on the things above, not on the things on the earth (Colossians 3:2) by exercising our minds, thinking **His** thoughts. Thinking His thoughts transfers power that gives us an authentic experience of spiritual maturity—the mind of Christ. When we are full of God's power, we can do all He asks of us to fulfill purpose and destiny and not miss any godly assignments. Christ has made us new creations; therefore, letting go of the hold we have on the past is necessary to keep the mind of Christ.

Reflection Questions

1. What thoughts do you often hold on to from the past, even though you know Christ has given you a new life?
2. What are you going to do to change this habit?

Warfare Prayer

I **uproot** and take authority over every spirit of disorder in my mind now. In the name of Jesus. I **eliminate** it now and send Holy Ghost fire to every assignment of mental clutter, for Your Word says You are a God of peace and not disorder. I **stomp out** disorder from my mind and declare I am sober-minded, disciplined, and committed to controlling my thoughts and emotions. I declare I am productive and operate in purpose. The Lord establishes the steps of a man, and He delights in His way (Psalm 37:23-24), so I align my thoughts and ways to Yours, God. I **sever** my life completely free from stagnancy, procrastination, and any mind-blinding spirit. I declare my mind stays on Christ, and my labor produces energy in the name of Jesus (Romans 8:6). I am not merely a dreamer, but I am a person of action. I release the grace of consistency and diligence over me. In the name of Jesus. I declare the finisher's anointing over me, and I **bind** all backlash and retaliation. In Jesus' name. Amen.

Day 30
Blazing Trails
by Dr. Cubeon Washington

"I have strength for all things in Christ Who empowers me [I am ready for anything and equal to anything through Him Who [a]infuses inner strength into me; I am [b]self-sufficient in Christ's sufficiency]" (Philippians 4:13, AMPC).

Walking in the fullness of who God has called you to be will require you to "step out of the boat" like the apostle Peter, figuratively speaking. Everything seems impossible until it suddenly is not. When I think about the seemingly impossible assignments God has given me, I often remind myself that walking on the moon was once seemingly impossible too. Walking on the moon was not impossible. It just had not been done before Neil Armstrong in 1969. Too often, we mistakenly categorize things as impossible simply because we have not seen it done before. Just because something has never been done before does not mean it cannot be done.

This is important for every trailblazer to keep in mind because unfortunately, you do not have a blueprint to follow. When you are a trailblazer, you are the blueprint others will later have the blessing and comfort of following. Where does the comfort of the trailblazer come from? The trailblazer's comfort comes from Holy Spirit, our Comforter and Counselor, who teaches us whatever it is we need to know (John 14:26).

Sometimes the trail you are blazing may not be new in the earth realm, but it is new within your bloodline, community, or sphere of influence. In these instances, the trail you are blazing still requires the comfort and direction of Holy Spirit to accomplish your mission. Close communion with God is necessary because our enemy satan and his demonic kingdom are working to keep you from fulfilling your destiny.

One of the most significant battles you will face as a trailblazer is the battle of your mind. Satan and his cohort of evil spirits will attempt to fill your mind with doubt and unbelief. The enemy's purpose is to make you believe you are insignificant, and God can't use you to accomplish something great. I personally have had to battle thoughts of inferiority and fear. However, my weapon of choice in this battle is speaking the Word of God. Staying in close communion with the Holy Spirit helps me remain calm and confident in blazing trails on the earth, bloodline, and sphere of influence. Staying in close communion with Holy Spirit and speaking the Word of God will help you be all God has called you to be as well.

Reflection Questions

1. Consider this: who are we to say we can't do something when God almighty says we can? Do you know better than God?
2. What do you feel Holy Spirit leading you to do that you feel inferior and incapable of doing?

Warfare Prayer

I talk and walk confidently in my kingdom assignments because my steps are ordered by God (Psalm 37:23). I **cripple** spirits of insecurity, inferiority, and timidity. I **strip** them of their power in my mind. The righteous are bold as a lion (Proverbs 28:1). By the power of my Lord and Savior Jesus Christ, I **assassinate** the spirit of fear and rejection. Their power is **made void** by the blood of Jesus. Like Jesus, whatever I **curse** at the root is **destroyed** and shall never live or bear fruit again. Demonic assignments of insecurity, inferiority, timidity, and fear shall never bear fruit in my life again. God has not given me a spirit of fear but of power, love, and a sound mind (2 Timothy 1:7). Everything I touch turns into prophetic gold and prospers. I decree and declare I can do all things through Christ who gives me strength (Philippians 4:13). His strength is made perfect in my weakness (2 Corinthians 12:9). I decree and declare there will be no backlash or retaliation. In the name of Jesus. Amen.

Day 31
Married but Broken
by Monica Williams

"A capable, intelligent, and [a] virtuous woman-who is he who can find her? She is far more precious than jewels, and her value is far above rubies or pearls" (Proverbs 31:10, AMPC).

I was born and raised in the heart of the Mississippi Delta. Success in life and my value as a young woman seemed directly tied to whether or not I was married. It seemed the earlier you got married, the more valuable you were. I recall going away to college and returning home to these dreaded questions: "Are you married yet? When are you getting married? Isn't it time for you to get married?" The fact that I'd done well in my studies and landed a good job after graduation didn't seem to matter nearly as much as the fact that I was still unmarried. No consideration was given to the fact that I could not marry myself. No, someone had to ask me. This issue was totally outside my control.

Finally, I was married and could breathe a sigh of relief. It wasn't until my marriage disintegrated under the pressures of life that I was reminded of just how important "marriage" was. I realized my value as a person, identity, and self-worth was tied to whether I was married. I'd never experienced being alone. Fear and anxiety gripped me, and even though I was a mother of two beautiful young adults who loved me dearly and needed support and guidance, I felt diminished as a person and worthless if I wasn't married. I hadn't realized "marriage" had become an idol; it was in the place reserved for God. Whether I was prepared for marriage, the condition of my marriage, and the spiritual, emotional health of my marriage took a back seat behind the throne of just being married. I'd lost my dad some years earlier, and now, my broken emotional state told me there was no one to tell me I had value and worth; I was beautiful or loved. The enemy highlighted all I didn't have and told me there wasn't any reason to live.

I'd expected being married would fix all that was missing and broken inside me! This was far from the truth. I was married and still broken. I learned marriage could not fix the brokenness I had brought with me into the marriage. What was needed was an inside job. I had a God-sized empty space that man could never fill. I had to rely on God for healing and deliverance totally. Fortunately, God was right there. He led me to His Word and to understand who I was as His child. As I walked out my healing and deliverance, He revealed why I was created: for His divine purpose. I was created to be a helper, comforter, advocate, intercessor, strengthener, adviser, and one who stands in the unconditional love of God. I was created to be the hands, feet, and voice of God whether I was single or married. I studied His Word and began to see myself as God sees me. I am His beautiful creation, fearfully and uniquely made, far more valuable than rubies and pearls.

Reflection Question

Who (or what) is sitting on the throne of your life? If your answer is not God, what steps do you need to take to be in right standing with God?

Warfare Prayer

Father God, in the mighty name of Jesus, I **demolish** every idol that has been erected in my life to misalign, misguide, and distract me from knowing who You created me to be. I **renounce** all generational curses of idolatry and strongholds of witchcraft in my bloodline and family, which has caused us to abort the plans You have for us and keep us from fulfilling our God-given destinies and purpose. I **expose** every plot, plan, and trick of the enemy that seeks to conceal my identity and diminish my value and worth to the kingdom of heaven. I **crush** the head of the serpents of low self-esteem, low self-worth, and loss of identity with my heel, and send Holy Ghost fire to burn them to ashes. The enemy's weapons of worthlessness, despair, lost identity, not knowing who I am and whose I am or why I was created will form but will not prosper! I am a son/daughter and heir of the Most High God! I did not choose You, but You chose me! I put no other gods before You. You are my Jehovah Jireh, more than enough. I am complete in You; I need not look for any other. I am fearfully and wonderfully made. I am a helper, capable, wise, and virtuous. My value is more precious than jewels, and my worth is far above rubies or pearls. This is Your Holy Word concerning me, and I am in covenant with You, God, through the finished work of Christ on the cross. I **bind** all backlash and retaliation! You have given me the keys of the kingdom, and whatever I bind on the earth will be bound in heaven, and whatever I loose on the earth will be loosed in heaven. In the matchless name of Jesus. Amen.

Helpmeet Army Co-Authors

After the reconciliation and ultimate restoration of my marriage, God began to open the door for me to mentor and coach others in marriage through my testimony. Through struggles, God revealed to me that to overcome, not only my marital problems and immaturity in God, I had to become a Helpmeet that was suitable for my King and learn to be a warrior in the spirit realm. It was then I learned how to use my weapons of warfare skillfully. It changed my marriage, helped me create an atmosphere that was conducive for my husband Gerald's deliverance, and I healed from traumas in my past and bloodline. The weapons against us did not prosper.

God said, "I'm releasing you to raise an Army of Helpmeets. I want you to train others as I trained you. I want them to be strong enough to win the battle for their freedom and the freedom of their families." Basically, God gave me the green light to build what is now the Helpmeet Army Mentoring program.

Some have been promoted to not only become warriors themselves but to build their personal ministries and gifts while helping others become fierce and feminine!

Meet the 31 women of the SWAT (Spiritual Warfare Arsenal Training) team within the Helpmeet Army who have written a devotional about an area they have overcome. Along with sharing a part of their journey, they have written reflections for you to combat the enemy as well. As warriors, they know the power of warfare prayers and have provided those for each day!

Contributing Author Biographies

Amina Aboki-Thompson is a wife, mother, entrepreneur and career woman who resides in New York with her family. She currently oversees the youth ministry at her church, loves helping others and enjoys adventures and traveling with her family. You can learn more about Amina through her Facebook and Instagram pages.

Ashley Banks is the wife of Corey Banks and the mother of three girls. She is currently a stay-at-home mom and entrepreneur. Her website is mamabearnatural.net.

Marci L. Bond is the wife of Kendall Bond and founder of Path4Purpose Life Coaching. Marcia is a motivator, encourager, and passionate woman of God who wholeheartedly desires to help people pursue their purpose and live the lives God predestined for them. Individuals can connect by emailing Marcia_Bond@outlook.com.

Sukaena Callander is an author of the newly written book, Overcoming the Destiny Stealer, and An Overcomers Journal. She is the wife of Shane Callander, mother of 5, entrepreneur, and a powerful intercessor. You may contact her via her website: sandsglobalservice.com, email: sandsglobalservices@gmail.com, FB: Sukaena Callander, S and S Global Services, or IG @Sukaena Callander.

Stephanie Canton is the wife of Jadarien Canton Sr. She is a mother of three children, an ordained minister, author, and entrepreneur. She is the founder of GYLT Ministries, Inc. and Boss Chick 4The Kingdom. Her websites are gytlministries.org and ast2freedom.com.

Giovan Clifton is the wife of Lloyd Clifton and the mother of four children. She is an author, fitness coach, Zumba instructor, entrepreneur, and cup creator. She can be found on FB and IG under My Cup Runs Over LLC. and Real G Fitness.

Anja M. Collins *is a Kingdom Ambassador, worshiper and writer. It is Anja's passion and joy to encourage God's daughters to live life in the fullness God has created for them. You can find Anja at www.anjamaia.com.*

Khatarrie Durden *is married to her King Braylen Durden. Together they have two children. She is a wife, mother, Army Veteran, teacher, and entrepreneur. She can be contacted at genuinelyher@gmail.com.*

Mary Elam *is the wife of Ricky Elam and the mother of four children and GiGi to five grandchildren. She is a bestselling author, intercessor, preacher, teacher, certified Wisdom Coach, prophetic voice, and entrepreneur. Her website is www.touchinghishem.com.*

Michelle Engles *is the wife of Jason Engles and homeschool mom of three sons. She is co-owner of Anchored Properties, LLC. and Dirt Road Logistics, LLC and a brand partner for Young Living Essential Oils. You can find her on Facebook and Instagram.*

Dr. Katrina Foster *is the wife of Timothy Foster and the proud mother of one son. She is a writer, author, editor, school principal, and teacher. She can be reached at drkatrinafoster@gmail.com.*

Hiyasmin Harper *is a wife, daughter, and woman after God's heart. She currently is the SVP of Accounting for a Real Estate Investment Firm in Los Angeles.*

 **Shalenie Hunter** is a wife and mother of two amazing children. She is a behavioral therapist, worshiper, dancer, and motivator. Her website is www.unwindwithshalenie.com.

 **Janelle Hutcheson** is a fun enthusiast who enjoys using her time to assist and bring joy to others. She is passionate about life and is dedicated to leaving an impeccable legacy that her children will be proud of and carry on. In her spare time, she pursues activities that allow her to create unforgettable memories. She can be reached at Janelle.hutcheson@gmail.com.

 **Maxine Baker Jackson** is the wife of DeVon S. Jackson and the mother of three children. Max is an author, mentor/coach for women and youth, prophetic intercessor, praise and worship minister, and entrepreneur. She may be contacted at CoveringOurChildrenInc@gmail.com.

Tabitha Jones is the wife of Jonathan Jones and mother of five children. She is a prophet, minister, musician, songwriter, and teacher of the Word. Her website is Cinda25sweet@yahoo.com.

Bejahda Lovelace is a daughter of the Most High God, mother, teacher, singer, and entrepreneur. She can be reached at tiktok.com/@forthekingdom2.

Kelley McLean is a wife, mom, growth strategist, business coach, and entrepreneur. She loves helping ambitious Christian women discover, start, and monetize their purpose projects. She's also co-founder of The Hope Ambassadors with her husband Torres where they help their clients close the gap between where they are currently and where God is calling them.

Website: www.thehopeambassadors.com.

Chalonda McQueen *is the wife of Roosevelt F. McQueen and mother of four children. She is a Lead Sales Merchandiser and Certified Trainer at Frito-Lay/PepsiCo. You can reach her on FB and IG @SweetestCandy76.*

Melinda Nicholson *is a Helpmeet Suitable, devoted mother of two adult children and proud grandmother of two adorable granddaughters. She is an Operations Director, trainer, mentor, and Independent Paparazzi Consultant with a BS in Business Administration and a MS in Management. Melinda's email address is melindadnicholson@gmail.com.*

Tabetha Pittman *is the wife of Jerome Pittman and the mother of Niketa and Jerome "Kidd" Pittman, Mink Mink of one grand man, Marshawn. She is an author, teacher, leader, notary, motivational speaker, and is in training to be a counselor and entrepreneur. Her websites are www.touchoftab.com and www.tabonthemove.com.*

Nikki Purcell is the wife of Robert Purcell and has two amazing young men Roshiem and Nicholas Purcell. She has the heart to serve others and loves to worship. She can be found on FB as Nikki Alston Purcell.

Alkesha Rogers is a wife and mother of six. She is a Registered Nurse Case Manager and self-taught cake decorator. Alkesha enjoys managing her home bakery in her spare time. Her website site is treatzcouture@gmail.com.

Rose Rome Hammond is a woman after God's own heart as she honors the Lord, as a Helpmeet to her husband, and an example to her blended family of eight children three sons-in-love and 14.5 grandchildren in love. She has been an administrative professional in the private, non-profits, and local government sectors for the last forty years and is also an entrepreneur and aspiring author. She can be reached at rose.rome51@gmail.com.

Carla Shelton lives in Houston, Texas. She is a mother, mentor, and multifaceted entrepreneur. Carla can be reached at cshelton@cnjholdingsgroup.com.

Nequia Speaks is an experienced Master Level Clinician. She is a mentor to youth, author, and facilitator of marriage small groups. Nequia is the proud mother of two beautiful daughters, the absolute love of Alexander Speaks' life. You can reach her by emailing nequiaspeaks@yahoo.com.

Wykehlia Stanley is the wife of Donnie Stanley and a mother. She currently works in the healthcare field and is a yielded vessel of Christ. She can be reached at mrsstanley14@gmail.com.

Darlene Staring *is the wife of Eric Staring and mother of 2 children. She is an entrepreneur, a Helpmeet suitable, and faith warrior.*

Vonda Warren *is the wife of Joshua Warren and a mother of two children. She provides virtual home and office organizing consultation services, including balance, planning, and time management. Her website is kingdomkeysoflife.com.*

Dr. Cubeon Washington *is the wife of Addison Washington. She is a well-respected prophetic voice, prophetic life coach, empowerment specialist and founder of Helpmeet Prep Academy. More information about Dr. Cubeon can be found on her website DrCubeon.com.*

Monica Williams *is a Helpmeet Suitable, a mother of two talented adults and Nana to three beautiful granddaughters. She is a Senior Civilian Army Leader, entrepreneur, co-author and motivational speaker. Her website is finallyfree.info, and her email address is finallyfree0801@gmail.com.*

About the Author

Yvette Benton is an apostolic voice with a Deborah anointing. She is anointed to not only pray but also train other Helpmeets to pray and believe God's Word for their marriages, families, and destinies. She and her husband Gerald have a testimony of marriage restoration through unconditional love and the power of spiritual warfare prayers. They have been married for over 21 years and now have a unique team ministry. Their marriage ministry Gerald & Yvette Ministries (GYM) teaches the body of Christ how to fulfill the roles of a Priest, Prophet, King (PPK), and a Helpmeet suitable. This is the foundation of a kingdom family.

Contact Yvette Benton

Contact Yvette Benton on their various social media platforms:

Facebook: Gerald and Yvette Ministries

YouTube: Gerald and Yvette Ministries

Instagram: @Gym_Ministries

Twitter: @GeraldandYvette

Website: www.GeraldandYvette.com

Email: Geraldandyvette@gmail.com

Made in USA - Crawfordsville, IN
39580_9781734633535
03.22.2022 1233